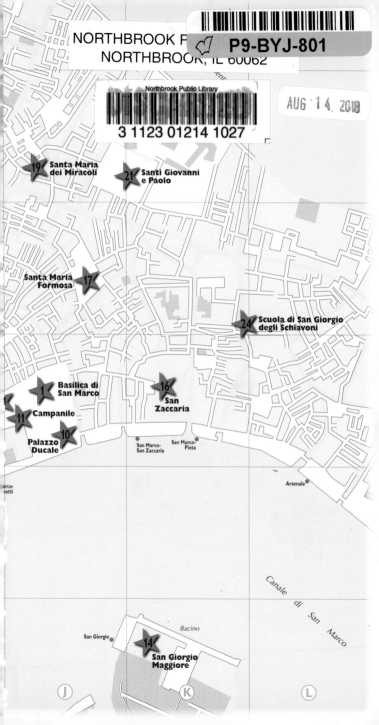

19 Santa Maria
dei Miracoli

21 Santi Giovanni
e Paolo

17 Santa Maria
Formosa

24 Scuola di San Giorgio
degli Schiavoni

1 Basilica di
San Marco

16 San
Zaccaria

11 Campanile

10 Palazzo
Ducale

San Marco-
San Zaccaria

San Marco-
Pieta

arco-
ietti

Arsenale

Canale di San Marco

Bacino

San Giorgio

14 San Giorgio
Maggiore

J

K

L

Fodor's
25 Best

VENICE

Contents

KEY TO SYMBOLS

- ✚ Map reference to the accompanying pull-out map
- ✉ Address
- ☎ Telephone number
- ◉ Opening/closing times
- 🍴 Restaurant or café
- 🚉 Nearest rail station
- 🚍 Nearest bus route
- ⛴ Nearest riverboat or ferry stop

🖐 Facilities for visitors with disabilities
🄸 Tourist information
❓ Other practical information
▷ Further information

💷 Admission charges:
Expensive (over €9),
Moderate (€6–€9) and
Inexpensive (under €6)

Introducing Venice

Venice has been seducing visitors for centuries, its impossible watery setting and fairy-tale appearance casting a spell whose potency remains undiminished by floods, mass tourism and the many other travails of the modern world.

The city sits at the heart of a lagoon, its many islands, alleys and canals divided into six districts, or *sestieri*, three to the west of the Canal Grande (San Polo, Dorsoduro and Santa Croce) and three to the east (San Marco, Castello and Cannaregio). Each has its own unmissable sights and each has a maze of timeless alleys and streets—a delight to wander for their own sake.

This labyrinth may initially look intimidating, but the city is easier to navigate than it looks: Distances are short, a few key streets wend through the maze, and the Rialto, Venice's old commercial heart, and the Piazza San Marco, its most famous square, provide central points of reference. On your first morning, though, resist the temptation to dash for the major sights. Start instead with a cappuccino in a sleepy square, or something where the crowds don't turn you away from the city at the first acquaintance.

Then you can move to the bigger draws and finally grapple with what to see among Venice's plethora of wonderful churches, palaces and museums. Don't forget the cafés, walks, tiny shops and essential boat trips along the Canal Grande or perhaps out to the islands of the lagoon.

However, in seeing the sights, don't fall into the trap of believing Venice is a sort of medieval theme park, a dead city sustained for the benefit of visitors. The population may be falling, but this is an enduring place; a city where people live and work, raise their families and have the same hopes and worries as people everywhere else. Where they differ is in living their everyday lives surrounded by the glories of one of the world's most beautiful cities. The pride they feel in this manifests itself in very diverse ways, but it's indubitably this pride that will preserve the city and its treasures for generations to come.

FACTS AND FIGURES

● It is estimated that there are 3,000 alleys in Venice. Laid end to end they would stretch for 192km (120 miles)
● Venice has around 400 bridges
● The city has some 500 souvenir shops
● Fifty percent of the city's workforce is involved in tourism
● In 1946 the population of central Venice was 110,000; today, it's around 58,000

SPECIAL TICKETS

The Venezia Unica City Pass (€49.90, 6–29s €36.90) is valid for 7 days. It gives access to the Palazzo Ducale, Chorus Group churches, 10 civic museums, an audio-tour to the Fenice and free entry or reductions to many attractions. The San Marco pack (€37.90) is similar but only includes the museums in and around San Marco. Book online at veneziaunica.it.

ACQUA ALTA

Visit Venice between November and April and you run the risk of encountering *acqua alta* or "high water," when winter weather, winds and high tides combine to submerge large areas. Raised wooden walkways, *passerelle*, are laid out on key routes to help people get around, and packing some waterproof footwear is a good idea.

BEST MOMENTS

These are often away from the main sights. So take a boat along the Canal Grande just for the ride, or see the Rialto markets at the crack of dawn before the crowds arrive. Little beats an aerial view, preferably from the top of San Giorgio Maggiore, and no city offers more to those who wander at random. A trip to the islands off-season can be magical.

Focus On Venice in the 21st Century

With a solid thousand years of tourism under their belts, Venetians are used to reinventing their city's image and into the second decade of the new millennium, there's a feeling that once more the balance has shifted.

Visiting Venice

Today's tourists no longer have time to spend a couple of weeks gently exploring; more than 80 percent spend just one day in Venice, pouring into the city from trains, buses and the vast cruise liners whose presence is such a contentious issue for many locals. The others come for perhaps two or three days only, and all of them are more focused on catching the main sights, enjoying good eating and shopping, than ticking off obscure churches visited.

Saving the City

Given its watery peculiarities, Venice has its own problems if it's to function as a 21st-century city. For far too long, the state of the lagoon and the problems with pollution and flooding were ignored. This changed around 2000 when the vast civic engineering project known as MOSE was launched. Its best known feature is the huge pontoons, which will rise from the sea floor at the entrances into the lagoon at very high tides and protect the city from the regular flooding it still receives. These are due to be operational in 2018, but much of the project has already been implemented. Beaches and dunes have been restored and replanted, the sea walls along the Adriatic strengthened, low-lying quaysides raised, salt marshes reinstated all over the lagoon and 12 eroding islands stabilized.

The industrial complex of Marghera on the west edge of the lagoon has been cleaned up, helping cut the air and water pollution, and it's hoped that by the 2050s Venice will be as secure as possible from decay and floods.

Clockwise from top: A costumed couple walk near Piazza San Marco during Carnavale; boats taking part in the Regata Storica on the Canal Grande in

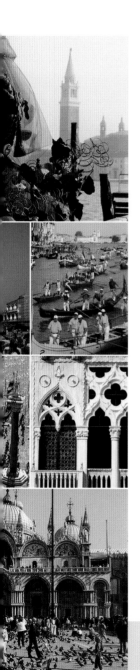

Getting it Right

Venetians and visitors need a city that really works, not a time capsule, and today, things simply function much better. IT has been enthusiastically embraced and tourists can now plan and book every aspect of their trip online before ever setting foot in Venice via the Venezia Unica app (▷ 163), which will also hold your hand while you're actually in the city.

Transport has greatly improved to help everyone get around, with the much-loved *vaporetti* (water buses) linking smoothly with buses, trains and a people-mover accessing the city's car parks, while the fourth Grand Canal bridge has changed commuters' lives for the better.

Eating and drinking habits have also changed considerably, and Venice now has modern, all-day eateries serving food that's right up to date alongside the more traditional places. The large student population ensures there are plenty of bars, many of which wouldn't look out of place in New York, London or Paris.

Experiences

Today, too, there's a lot more emphasis on the unique experiences that Venice can offer. Of course, there's the gondola ride and the high-end shopping, but there are also guided walks, behind-the-scenes visits to St Mark's Basilica, the Doge's Palace and the Fenice opera house, food and wine city tours or the chance to parade the streets in full 18th-century carnival costume—all captured for you on film. Visitors can learn to row Venetian-style, go jogging, swim in one of the city's pools or, around Christmas, enjoy the open-air ice rink in Campo San Polo.

Increasingly, tourists can create their own unique Venetian experience in a city facing the future with confidence.

September; a detail of the Gothic tracery on the facade of Ca' d'Oro; the striking Basilica di San Marco; Riva degli Schiavoni gondola pier; Piazza San Marco at night

Top Tips For

These great suggestions will help you tailor your ideal visit to Venice, no matter how you choose to spend your time.

Fabulous Views

Take the elevator to the top of the **Campanile** (▷ 34–35) for spectacular, far-reaching views over the rooftops.

The bell tower of **San Giorgio Maggiore** (▷ 40–41) offers sweeping vistas across the entire city.

Climb the tower of the cathedral on **Torcello** (▷ 62–63) for a sweeping panorama of the Venetian lagoon.

Burning the Midnight Oil

Have a drink in one of the cafés and bars on **Campo Santa Margherita** (▷ 67).

Find a fusty old *enoteca* (wine bar) such as **Do Mori** (▷ 136).

Venice has few late-opening nightspots—**Vino Vino** (▷ 139) and **Paradiso Perduto** (▷ 137) are two of the best.

The Lap of Luxury

Splash out on one of Venice's new-wave designer hotels—**Ca' Maria Adele** (▷ 157) typifies this fabulous self-indulgence.

Enjoy an expensive coffee or, better, an aperitif or late drink in **Caffè Florian** (▷ 147), a Venetian institution.

Experience the finest selection of luxury shopping in the sumptuous surroundings of the **Fondaco dei Tedeschi** (▷ 125).

A Breath of Fresh Air

Have a picnic or unwind in the grassy, tree-shaded **Giardini Savorgnan** (▷ 68).

Visit **Torcello** (▷ 62–63) for some bracing sea air.

Verdant **Sant'Erasmo** (▷ 76), Venice's vegetable garden, offers great opportunities for fresh air and country walking.

Clockwise from top: A view down onto Piazza San Marco from the Campanile; Canal Grande seen from the Ponte dell'Accademia; inside a shop selling

Keeping the Children Happy

Take them on plenty of boat rides, especially down the **Canal Grande** (▷ 20–21).
Buy them a mask from **Tragicomica** (▷ 129) or ice cream from **Nico** (▷ 149) or **GROM** (▷ 148).
Visit one of **Murano's glass factories** to see glassblowers in action (▷ 28–29).

Saving for a Rainy Day

Invest in the **San Marco pack Citypass** (€27.90) which gives access to the Palazzo Ducale, three civic museums, three Chorus churches and offers reductions to a number of other city attractions.
Travel the length of the **Canal Grande**, surely the world's finest journey by public transportation (▷ 20–21, 166–167).
Just €0.60 on a ***traghetto*** (▷ 167) across the Canal Grande buys you a ride on a gondola.

Specialty Shopping

Many of Venice's high-fashion and other designer stores cluster in and around Calle Larga XXII Marzo, or head for **Venetia Studium** (▷ 129) for the beautiful damasks, silks and velvets.
Nothing beats the **Rialto markets** (▷ 39, 128) and the delicatessens in the surrounding streets such as Ruga Vecchia di San Giovanni.
Small, specialist stores line the **Mercerie** (▷ 69) and other streets between St. Mark's and the Rialto Bridge. Marbled paper, glass and local foods are popular choices.

An Evening on the Town

Take in an opera or concert at **La Fenice** (▷ 75, 138), Venice's opera house.
Contact the tourist office (▷ 167) to find **a concert** in one of Venice's churches or palaces.
Dress up for an evening's lighthearted gambling in Venice's **casino** (▷ 135).

handmade paper; a fruit stall at the Rialto market; Teatro La Fenice; the sumptuous surroundings of Caffè Florian; the green fields on Torcello island

Timeline

800BC Sporadic settlement of the lagoon by the Venetii and Euganei tribes.

250BC Rome conquers Venetia and founds important colonies at Padua, Verona, Altinium and Aquileia.

MARCO POLO

Born in Venice in 1254, Marco Polo left with his father in 1269 on a journey that would last two decades. In 1275 he arrived at the court of Kublai Khan, where he served the Mongol emperor until 1295. In 1298 he was captured by the Genoese and it was from prison that he dictated his *Description of the World*.

ANTONIO VIVALDI

Vivaldi was born in Venice in 1678. Although ordained as a priest, he devoted his life to music, teaching violin at La Pietà orphanage, whose girls received music training as part of their state-funded education. La Pietà's orchestra enabled Vivaldi to create a wealth of musical compositions, including his most famous work *The Four Seasons*.

AD402 Alaric the Goth sacks Altinium and other northeastern colonies. A vision of the Virgin guides refugees to an island in the lagoon.

421 According to legend Venice is founded on 25 March, the Feast Day of the Virgin Mary.

453 Aquileia is sacked by Attila the Hun, prompting another exodus of refugees to the lagoon.

697 The first Doge (leader) of Venice, Paoluccio Anafesto, is elected.

810 Lagoon dwellers gather on the more easily defended islands of the Rialto.

828 Venetian merchants steal the relics of St. Mark from Alexandria.

1171 Venice's six districts are founded.

1204 Venice sacks Constantinople and acquires much of the former Byzantine Empire.

The Doge sets out in the Bucentaur *for the ceremony of Marriage to the Sea (▷ 162)*

Piazza San Marco after flooding

1380 Victory over the Genoese at the Battle of Chioggia. Venice wins naval supremacy in the Adriatic and Mediterranean.

1406 Venice defeats Padua and Verona to lay the foundations of a mainland empire.

1453 Venice's power is at its height but the Turks take Constantinople. Over the next 200 years they take Cyprus and Crete.

1498 The discovery of the Cape route to the East weakens Venice's trading monopolies.

1718 Loss of Morea marks the end of Venice's maritime empire.

1797 Napolean invades Italy: the last Doge abdicates and the Venetian Republic comes to an end.

1814 After Napoleán's defeat, the Congress of Vienna cedes Venice and the Veneto to Austria.

1866 Venice joins a united Italy.

1966 Devastating floods draw international attention to the decay of Venice's buildings and artistic treasures; start of major fund-raising for restoration.

2007 Ponte della Costituzione, bridge over Canal Grande, opens.

2012 Annual tourist numbers top 17,250,000; city population falls below 58,000.

2018 MOSE flood barrier due to become operational.

COURTESANS AND VENETIAN GREED

At the end of the 16th century, the city contained 11,654 women of the night. This compared with 2,889 patrician women, 1,936 burghers and 2,508 nuns. Taxes from prostitution funded an estimated 12 ships. In the 18th century, according to one contemporary report, "Venetians did not taste their pleasures, but swallowed them whole." Another observer wrote that "the men are women, the women are men, and all are monkeys."

Marco Polo, the great Venetian-born traveler

Crossing Ponte della Costituzione

Top 25

This section contains the must-see Top 25 sights and experiences in Venice. They are listed alphabetically, and numbered so you can locate them on the inside front cover map.

1 Basilica di San Marco

- Central door
- Facade mosaics
- Bronze horses
- Rood screen
- Mosaic pavement
- Pala d'Oro
- Interior mosaics

- Dress code: no shorts; women must cover shoulders and upper arms.
- To avoid long lines go in early or late afternoon.

The perfect architectural fusion of east and west, the great Basilica di San Marco, glittering with mosaics, embodies the might of medieval Venice and the skill of its builders.

St. Mark's resting place The basilica was begun in 832 to house the body of St. Mark, stolen from Alexandria by Venetian merchants four years earlier. For almost 1,000 years it served as the doge's private "chapel" and the city's spiritual heart, accumulating the decorative fruits of a millennium to emerge as the most exotic hybrid of Western and Byzantine architecture in Europe. The original building (destroyed by rioting) was replaced in 978 and again in 1094, the church from the latter date making up most of the one you see today.

Clockwise from far left: The decorated facade above the main door of the basilica; the interior is decorated with mosaics depicting the basilica itself; the basilica lit up at night-time; a rooftop detail of the Winged Lion, a symbol of St. Mark

Time to explore Admiring the basilica's treasures is exhausting because there are so many, and because the almost constant crowds can make exploring a challenge. The building remains overwhelmingly striking; spend a few minutes taking in some of the exterior details before plunging inside. These include the *Translation of the Body of St. Mark to the Basilica* (1260–70) above the leftmost door, the west facade's only original mosaic (the rest are later copies) and the superb Romanesque carvings (1240–65) above the central door. Inside, see the famous bronze horses (probably third century AD) in the upper gallery, the view from the Loggia dei Cavalli, the treasury (full of antique silverware), and the Pala d'Oro, an altar screen encrusted with more than 2,600 pearls, rubies, emeralds and other precious stones.

THE BASICS

basilicasanmarco.it
🚹 J6
✉ Piazza San Marco 1, San Marco 30124
☎ 041 270 8311
🕐 Apr–Oct Mon–Sat 9.45–5, Sun 2–5; Nov–Mar 9.45–4.30, Sun 2–4
🍴 Piazza San Marco
🚢 All services to San Marco Vallaresso, San Marco Giardinetti or San Zaccaria
♿ Some steps; uneven floors
💶 Basilica free. Treasury and Pala d'Oro expensive

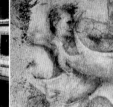

HIGHLIGHTS

● Canal Grande facade
● *Massacre of the Innocents*, artist unknown
● *Crucifixion*, Antonio Vivarini
● *St. Sebastian*, Andrea Mantegna
● *Man and Woman*, busts by Tullio Lombardo
● *The Story of the True Cross*, bronze reliefs by Andrea Briscio
● *Madonna*, Giovanni Bellini
● *Flagellation*, Luca Signorelli

The smaller and less famous galleries of a city are often the most rewarding. The Ca' d'Oro's collection of paintings, sculptures and objets d'art is one of the most absorbing in Venice.

Palace The Ca' d'Oro, or "House of Gold," takes its name from the gilding that once covered its facade, a decorative veneer now worn away by wind and rain. However, the facade remains one of the most accomplished pieces of Venetian-Byzantine architecture in the city. The same, sadly, cannot be said of the interior, which has been much altered over time.

Exhibits Galleria Franchetti, named for the owner who gave his home and collection to the state in 1916, divides into two floors, each

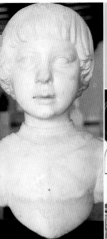

Clockwise from far left: The remarkable exterior of Ca' d'Oro; the bust of a young boy, dating from the 15th century, by Giovanni Romano; people looking out onto the canal from the loggia; a detail of Cacciata del Paradiso by Giovanni de Sacchis (16th century)

arranged around a central *portego*. On the lower floor a captivating polyptych of the *Crucifixion* by Antonio Vivarini greets you, along with sculptural fragments belonging to the *Massacre of the Innocents* (14th century). Moving right you come to the gallery's pictorial masterpiece, Mantegna's sombre *St. Sebastian* (1506). To its left, in the *portego*, is a pair of busts by Tullio Lombardo (15th century), followed by six bronze reliefs, *The Story of the True Cross*, by Andrea Briscio (1470–1532). The rooms off the *portego* contain medallions, a Madonna by Giovanni Bellini and a range of Florentine and Sienese paintings.

More art Upstairs there are tapestries, paintings by Titian, Van Dyck and Tintoretto, and damaged frescoes by Pordenone, Titian and Giorgione.

THE BASICS

polomuseale.venezia.
beniculturali.it

➕ G4

✉ Calle di Ca' d'Oro, Cannaregio 3932, off Strada Nova

☎ 041 522 2349

🕐 Mon 8.15–2, Tue–Sun 8.15–7.15

🚇 Ca' d'Oro N, 1

♿ Poor: stairs

✋ Moderate

HIGHLIGHTS

- Ballroom
- G.B. Tiepolo ceiling frescoes
- Carrera portraits
- Lacquerwork
- Gondola cabin, or *felze*
- Canaletto paintings
- Francesco Guardi paintings
- Pietro Longhi paintings
- G.D. Tiepolo satirical frescoes

If you want a taste of the opulent lifestyle enjoyed by the aristocracy inside a Grand Canal *palazzo*, take a boat to Ca' Rezzonico, once one of the city's most magnificent private houses, now a museum devoted to life, art and style in 18th-century Venice.

How it began The Ca' Rezzonico was begun in 1667 by Baldassare Longhena, a leading architect of his day, but remained half-finished. In 1751 the shell was bought by the Rezzonico family and passed through several hands before opening as a museum in 1936. It begins in fine style in the sumptuous ballroom with *trompe-l'œil* and huge chandeliers. Highlights of rooms include ceiling frescoes by G.B. Tiepolo, fine lacquerwork, Flemish tapestries and pastel portraits by Rosalba Carrera.

Left: Detail of The Banquet at Casa Nani, Given in Honor of their Guest, Clemente Augusto, Elector Archbishop of Cologne, on 9th September 1755 *by Pietro Longhi in the gallery's collection; below: The exterior of the building seen from the Canal Grande*

The collection Much of the palace is devoted to a picture gallery, whose highlight is some paintings by Canaletto, three of only a handful that remain on public display in Venice. Also of interest are Francesco Guardi's views of the city's convents and gambling rooms, together with 39 amateurish but fascinating portraits of Venetian life by Pietro Longhi. Among them is his well-known *Rhinoceros*, painted during the animal's stay in Venice in 1779. Rooms off to the right include a splendid bed-chamber, complete with 18th-century closet and sponge-bag. Of special note are a series of satirical frescoes (1793–97) by G.D. Tiepolo, a collection of traditional puppets, three rooms from an old pharmacy, fine clothing enhanced with lace and the excellent views from the palace's upper floors.

THE BASICS

carezzonico.visitmuve.it
E6
Fondamenta Rezzonico, Dorsoduro 3136
041 241 0100
Apr–Oct Wed–Mon 10–6; Nov–Mar 10–5. Ticket office closes 1 hour earlier
Campo San Barnaba
Ca' Rezzonico 1
Good
Expensive
City Pass (▷ 4)

4 Canal Grande

- Palazzo Vendramin-Calergi
- San Stae
- Ca' Pesaro (▷ 66–67)
- Ca' d'Oro (▷ 16–17)
- Ponte di Rialto
- Ca' Rezzonico (▷ 18–19)
- Santa Maria della Salute (▷ 52–53)

TIPS

- The *vaporetto* is probably the best way of seeing the canal; gondolas and taxis are far more expensive.
- If time is short take the No. 2, which has fewer stops than the No. 1.

The world's most beautiful "street" offers an endlessly unfolding pageant with superb views of the city's finest palaces and a fascinating insight into Venetian life.

A riot of life and noise Snaking 4km (2.5 miles) through the heart of Venice, it divides the city: Three of the city's six districts, or *sestieri*, lie to one side and three to the other. For much of the day and night it is alive with boats and bustle, providing an almost hypnotic spectacle when admired from one of its four bridges (Costituzione, Scalzi, Rialto and Accademia) or from the heavily laden *vaporetti* that ply up and down the canal. In addition to the life of the canal is the attraction of the palaces that line its banks, a historical digest of the city's most appealing architecture dating back

Far left: A busy stretch along the Canal Grande; middle: Lights sparkle on the waters on the canal; below: Looking along the canal past striped gondola poles towards Santa Maria della Salute

over 500 years. From the Ponte di Rialto, Venice's most famous bridge, you get a view of the canal at its most frantically busy.

Jump on board A trip along this intriguing canal is a pleasure in itself. Board *vaporetto* No. 1 or No. 2 at Piazzale Roma or the Ferrovia (rail station), making sure the boat is heading in the right direction. For the best views, try to secure one of the few outside seats at the front or rear of some boats: Venetians prefer to stand in the middle. The Rialto and Accademia bridges make convenient breaks in the ride, but for your first trip go all the way to San Marco (and then do the return trip to take in the glory of the palaces on the opposite bank). It is also well worth making the trip at night, when the experience, if anything, is even more magical.

THE BASICS

✚ D4–G7

🚢 1, 2 (year-round)

♿ Good

🖐 Moderate

❓ *Vaporetto* 1 halts at every stop; 2 stops at Piazzale Roma, Ferrovia, San Marcuola, Rialto, Sant'Angelo, San Tomà, San Samuele, Accademia, San Marco Vallaresso and San Marco Giardinetti

5 Collezione Peggy Guggenheim

HIGHLIGHTS

● The New Wing
● Henry Moore sculptures
● *Bird in Space*, Constantin Brancusi
● *Red Tower*, De Chirico
● *Robing of the Bride*, Max Ernst
● Silver bedhead, Alexander Calder
● Jackson Pollock paintings
● *The Poet*, Pablo Picasso
● *Angel of the Citadel*, Marino Marini

A unique and unfinished *palazzo* on the Canal Grande, one of Venice's top visitor attractions, is home to a superb collection of mid-20th-century modern art, imaginatively displayed both indoors and outside.

Perfect setting The Guggenheim's small but polished collection was accumulated by Peggy Guggenheim (1898–1979), daughter of an American copper magnate, and installed by her in the 18th-century Palazzo Venier dei Leoni. The collection's appeal owes much to its immaculate presentation as well as to the beauty of its setting, many of the sculptures being arranged in a lovely garden. This has works by Henry Moore, Paolozzi, Giacometti and others, and houses the New Wing and appealing museum store.

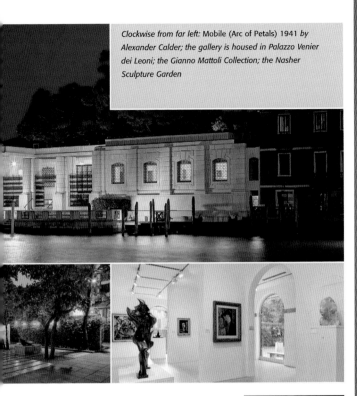

Clockwise from far left: Mobile (Arc of Petals) 1941 by Alexander Calder; the gallery is housed in Palazzo Venier dei Leoni; the Gianno Mattoli Collection; the Nasher Sculpture Garden

Modern art Guggenheim's taste and money allowed her to select high-quality works from virtually every modern-art movement of the 20th century. At the same time she had a penchant for the surreal and avant-garde, having enjoyed a brief relationship with the German surrealist painter Max Ernst. The collection features cubist works by Picasso and Braque, and the surrealism of Dalí, Magritte and Mirò. American modernists include Jackson Pollock and Mark Rothko, while the English are represented by Francis Bacon. There are sculptures by Calder and Brancusi, as well as works by Italian Futurists Balla and Boccioni from the Gianni Mattioli Collection. The most memorable work is Marino Marini's provocative *Angel of the Citadel*, on the terrace overlooking the Canal Grande.

THE BASICS

guggenheim-venice.it
🕀 G7
✉ Palazzo Venier dei Leoni, Calle San Cristoforo, Dorsoduro 704
☎ 041 240 5411
🕐 Wed–Mon 10–6
🚢 Salute 1
♿ Good
💷 Expensive

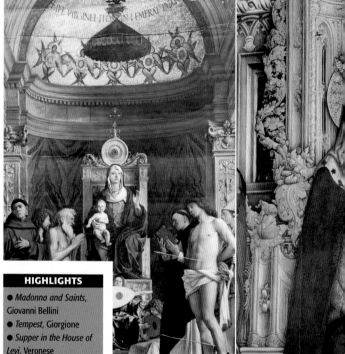

HIGHLIGHTS

● *Madonna and Saints,* Giovanni Bellini
● *Tempest,* Giorgione
● *Supper in the House of Levi,* Veronese
● *The Translation of the Body of St. Mark,* Tintoretto
● *Pietà,* Titian
● Pietro Longhi paintings
● *The Miracles of the True Cross*
● "Life of St. Ursula," Carpaccio

TIPS

● Try to avoid Sunday and arrive early if you can.
● English-language tours are available.
● Download the free app, Gallerie dell'Accademia, to make the most of your visit.

Art awaits you at every turn in this city, but you would miss a key experience without a visit to the Accademia, home to the world's greatest collection of Venetian paintings.

Masterpieces The Accademia began life as Venice's art school in 1750, moving to its present site in 1807 when it garnered much of its permanent collection from churches and religious houses suppressed by Napoleonic decree. The building combines ground-floor state-of-the-art, high-tech exhibition spaces with more traditional galleries above. Some of the gallery's best-known paintings are its Byzantine works, a style that influenced the city's earliest painters. Canvases by Carpaccio, Mantegna, Bellini and others reflect Venice's Renaissance heyday, alongside the Accademia's most

Clockwise from far left: Madonna and Child with Saints Francis, John the Baptist, Job, Dominic, Sebastian and Louis *by Giovanni Bellini; a detail of* Madonna and Child *by Antonio Vivarini; people waiting to enter the Gallerie; works by Tintoretto and Veronese in one of the rooms*

famous painting, Giorgione's *Tempest (c.*1500). High Renaissance masterpieces include Veronese's *Supper in the House of Levi* (1573) and Tintoretto's *Miracle of the Slave* and *The Translation of the Body of St. Mark (c.*1560).

Cycles Leave plenty of time for the Accademia's highlights, two *storie,* or fresco cycles. The first, *The Miracles of the True Cross* (1494–1510), was painted by a variety of artists for the Scuola di San Giovanni Evangelista. Each describes a miracle worked by a relic of the "True Cross" owned by the *scuola,* though often the miracle itself takes second place to the fascinating anecdotal detail. The same is true for the second cycle, painted by Carpaccio for the Scuola di Sant' Orsola, with episodes from the "Life of St. Ursula."

THE BASICS

gallerieaccademia.org

➕ F7

✉ Campo della Carità, Dorsoduro 1050

☎ 041 520 0345; reservations 041 250 0345

🕐 Tue–Sun 8.15–7.15, Mon 8.15–2

🍴 Campo Santo Stefano

🚤 Accademia 1, 2

♿ Poor: some steps

💶 Expensive

HIGHLIGHTS

- Facade
- Doorway
- *St. Christopher*, Nicolò di Giovanni
- Campanile
- *St. John the Baptist*, Cima da Conegliano
- *Presentation of the Virgin*, Tintoretto
- *The Making of the Golden Calf*, Tintoretto
- *Last Judgment*, Tintoretto
- *St. Agnes Raising Licinius*, Tintoretto (Cappella Contarini)

Madonna dell'Orto ranks high among the many superb Venetian churches. Its lovely setting, off the tourist trail, and graceful red-brick facade are complemented by an airy interior filled with appealing works of art.

Exterior The first church on the present site was founded in 1350 and dedicated to St. Christopher, a statue of whom still dominates the lovely brick and stone facade. The building was rededicated to the Virgin in 1377, an act that was inspired by a miracle-working statue of the Madonna found in a nearby vegetable garden *(orto)*. The elegant doorway, by Bartolomeo Bon, is a Renaissance-tinged work. Note the onion dome of the campanile, clear witness to the Byzantine influence on Venetian architecture.

Left: The brick and Istrian stone facade of the Madonna dell'Orto; below: Many of the paintings inside are by Tintoretto who, along with his children, is buried in the church

Interior grandeur Inside, the two aisles contain notable works. The artistic highlights begin in the Contarini Chapel above the first altar on the right, which has Cima da Conegliano's *St. John the Baptist* (1493). At the end of the right nave, above the door, stands Tintoretto's dramatic *Presentation of the Virgin* (1551). In the chapel to the right of the choir lies Tintoretto's tomb (he lived near the church), together with those of his children, Domenico and Marietta. A wall separates the artist from two of his finest paintings, the choir's grand *Last Judgment* and *The Making of the Golden Calf*. Of the three paintings in the apse to the rear, those on the right and left—the *Beheading of St. Paul* and *St. Peter's Vision of the Cross*—are by Tintoretto; the central *Annunciation* is by Palma il Giovane.

THE BASICS

chorusvenezia.org
✚ G2
✉ Campo Madonna dell'Orto, Cannaregio 3520
☎ 041 275 0462
🕐 Mon 10.30–4, Tue–Sat 10.30–4.30
🚤 Orto 4.1, 4.2, 5.1, 5.2
♿ Good
💰 Inexpensive
❓ Chorus Pass and City Pass (▷ 4)

HIGHLIGHTS

- Glass factories
- Museo del Vetro
- Santa Maria e Donato

The lagoon island of Murano is a miniature Venice, and has been the heart of Venetian glass production for over 800 years, its peak being between the 15th and 16th centuries.

Seeing Murano It's a 10-minute trip across the lagoon to Murano, a self-contained community with its own Canal Grande, fine churches, *palazzi* and glass-blowing industry. There are numerous privately run excursions from the city, but for good value and flexibility make the trip independently via the *vaporetti*. Allow two to three hours for a thorough visit. It's quite feasible, given an early start, to combine a visit to Murano with a trip to the northern islands of Burano and Torcello; study the *vaporetto* timetable with care as onward connections run half-hourly only.

Clockwise from left: A canal on the island of Murano; the colonnaded facade of the Basilica dei Santi Maria e Donato; a glass-making factory

Highlights The glass factories are well worth a visit but bear in mind the majority are closed on Saturday and Sunday. A glass-making hub since 1291, Murano has three major sights over and above its ubiquitous glass workshops and showrooms. The first is the church of San Pietro Martire noted for Giovanni Bellini's altarpiece. Also well worth seeing is the Museo del Vetro, Italy's only glass museum, with displays of objects dating from Roman times. Just beyond lies the church of Santa Maria e Donato, distinguished by a striking arched and colonnaded apse. Inside, the 12th-century apse mosaic of the Madonna is outstanding, as are the swirling tinted patterns of the lovely mosaic floor (1141). Don't miss the opportunity to visit a glass workshop or showroom, although you might be tempted by items on sale.

THE BASICS

⊕ b2
✉ Isola di Murano
🚤 N, 3, 4.1, 4.2, 12, 13, 18 from Piazzale Roma, Ferrovia and Fondamente Nove

Museo del Vetro
museovetro.visitmuve.it
⊕ b2
✉ Fondamenta Giustinian 8
☎ 041 527 4718
🕐 Apr–Oct daily 10–6; Nov–Mar 10–5. Ticket office closes 30 min earlier
🏛 Museo
💰 Expensive

Santa Maria e Donato
⊕ c2
✉ Campo San Donato
🕐 Mon–Sat 9–12, 3.30–7, Sun 3.30–7
🏛 Museo
💰 Free

HIGHLIGHTS

● Aerial view of Venice (1500), Jacopo de' Barbari
● *Daedalus and Icarus*, Canova
● *Two Women*, Carpaccio
● *The Man in the Red Hat*, Lorenzo Lotto (attributed)
● *Pietà*, Antonello da Messina
● *Madonna and Child*, Giovanni Bellini

Probably only a fraction of the visitors thronging Piazza San Marco venture into the Museo Correr. Those who do not are missing one of Venice's finest museums and picture gallery collections.

Fascinating overview Much of the collection here was accumulated by Abbot Teodoro Correr, a Venetian worthy, and bequeathed to the city in 1830. It was immediately housed in the buildings on the south side of Piazza San Marco, previously used as imperial apartments during the French occupation (1797–1814). Today, these sumptuous rooms form part of a visit, and lead to the key historic galleries, devoted to exhibits documenting Venetian history. Don't miss the Wunderkammer, displays of every type of exquisite objets d'art collected

Far left: A fresco of three dancing girls decorates the interior; middle: An impressive gallery; below: Doge Giovanni Mocenigo by Gentile Bellini (c.1478)

by 18th-century aristocrats. Also take time to visit the classical collections in the archeological section, or the superb Biblioteca Marciana, a library designed by Sansovino in 1591.

More art One of the main sections of the museum consists of a large hall devoted to several fine sculptures by Antonio Canova. Occupying the top floor is the city's second-finest art gallery after the Accademia. Its most popular picture is Carpaccio's *Two Women* (1507), a masterful study of ennui once known as *The Courtesans* for the plunging necklines. Other well-known paintings include *The Man in the Red Hat* (by either Carpaccio or Lorenzo Lotto) and a *Pietà* by Antonello da Messina, and works by Cosmè Tura, Alvise Vivarini, and Jacopo, Giovanni and Gentile Bellini.

THE BASICS

correr.visitmuve.it

🔢 H6

✉ Procuratie Nuove, Ala Napoleonica, Piazza San Marco 52, San Marco 30124

☎ 041 240 5211

🕐 Apr–Oct daily 10–7; Nov–Mar 10–5. Ticket office closes 1 hour earlier

🍴 Piazza San Marco

🚤 San Marco Vallaresso, San Marco Giardinetti N, 1, 2

♿ Poor

💷 Expensive

❓ City Pass (▷ 4)

HIGHLIGHTS

- Bridge of Sighs
- Tetrarchs
- Porta della Carta
- Scala dei Giganti
- Arco Foscari
- Sala dell'Anticollegio
- Sala del Collegio
- Sala del Maggior Consiglio
- Armory and prisons

TIP

- Winter visitors should dress warmly as there is no heating and it can be very cold.

Italy has a host of beautiful Gothic buildings, but the Palazzo Ducale is by far the most captivating: the seat of the doge and home to Venice's various offices of state for almost a thousand years.

Evolution The first ducal palace, completed in 814, was a severe fortress built on one of the few clay redoubts in the lagoon. This burned down in 976, as did its successor in 1106. By 1419 the palace was in its third—and final—incarnation. Three years later, the great hall, or Sala del Maggior Consiglio, was completed—one of many additions made to the interior. By 1550 most work had been completed, only to be undone by fires in 1574 and 1577, conflagrations that not only destroyed masterpieces by some of Venice's greatest painters,

Clockwise from far left: The Scala d'Oro (gold staircase) in the palazzo; a statue at the top of Scala dei Giganti; Ponte dei Sospiri (Bridge of Sighs); the astrological clock in the Sala Senato; a view along the outside of the building

but also threatened the entire building with collapse. Restoration work continued on and off until the 1880s.

Details Outside is the famous Ponte dei Sospiri (Bridge of Sighs), tucked down a canal at the palace's eastern end, and the fine corner sculptures. Don't miss the excellent carving of the pillars and capitals, and the palace's superb main doorway, the Porta della Carta (1438–43), with the famous little knights, or tetrarchs, to its left. An ornate staircase leads up several flights to the beginning of a marked route leading from one lavishly decorated room to the next. Look for works by Tintoretto, Veronese and other Venetian masters. Tintoretto's gargantuan *Paradiso* (1588–92), the world's largest oil painting, is in the Sala del Maggior Consiglio.

THE BASICS

palazzoducale.visitmuve.it

🔲 J6

✉ Piazzetta San Marco, San Marco 30124

☎ Palace and booking for guided tours 041 271 5911 or 041 4273 0892

🕐 Palace Apr–Oct daily 8.30–7; Nov–Mar 8.30–5.30. Ticket office closes 1 hour earlier

🍽 Palace café

🚤 All services to San Zaccaria, San Marco Vallaresso or San Marco Giardinetti

♿ Poor: steps to upstairs

💰 Expensive

❓ City Pass (▷ 4)

DID YOU KNOW?

● Number of Venetian towers in 1650: 200
● Number today: 170
● Number of Campanile bells: 5
● The Maleficio bell tolled during executions
● The Nona bell tolled at noon
● The Marangona bell tolled at the start and end of the working day
● All bells tolled at the election of a pope or doge
● Prisoners were hung in cages from the Campanile
● Elevator added in 1962

HIGHLIGHTS

Piazza
● Basilica di San Marco (▷ 14–15)
● Palazzo Ducale (▷ 32–33)
● Museo Correr (▷ 30–31)
● Procuratie
● Libreria Sansoviniana
● Torre dell'Orologio (▷ 75)
● Zecca
● Caffè Florian (▷ 147)

The Piazza San Marco is thronged throughout the day. Come early to avoid the crowds flocking to the Basilica, Palazzo Ducale and Campanile, or visit after midnight to have this wonderful space to yourself.

Hordes Europe's "drawing room" was how Napoleon described Venice's main square, though glancing at today's crowds he would probably be less complimentary. Arrive early or in the evening, however—or off-season—and the piazza can still work its considerable charms. Over and above the obvious sights and (expensive) cafés, make a point of taking in the Zecca (mint), the Procuratie (administrative offices), the underrated Museo Correr, and the Libreria Sansoviniana, considered one of the greatest buildings of its day. Also look for the

Far left: The view through an arch to Basilica di San Marco and the Campanile; middle: Looking down on the Piazzetta; below: From the Campanile there is a good view towards the island of Murano

Torre dell'Orologio (▷ 75) and notice the two granite columns on the waterfront besides the Palazzo Ducale.

Campanile Take the elevator up San Marco's detached bell tower for the views, which can stretch as far as the Alps. The original campanile, which at 98.5m (323ft) was the city's tallest building, dated from the 11th century. Erosion and shallow foundations (20m/66ft deep) proved the tower's undoing and, on 14 July 1902, it collapsed, though there were no casualties. It was rebuilt, as the Venetians insisted, *dov'era e com'era*—"where it was and how it was"—and opened on 25 April 1912, exactly 1,000 years after its predecessor. This time, though, it was 650 tons lighter and supported by an extra 1,000 foundation piles.

THE BASICS

basilicasanmarco.it
➕ H6–J6
🍴 Caffè Florian (▷ 147) and Quadri (▷ 83)
🚤 San Marco Vallaresso, San Marco Giardinetti N, 1, 2, 4, or all services to San Zaccaria
♿ Good
🏛 Museo Archeologico moderate
Campanile
basilicasanmarco.it
☎ 0141 522 4064
🕐 Easter to mid-Jun daily 9–7; mid-Jun to 5 Sep 8.30am–9.30pm; 6–18 Sep 8.30–8.15; 19–30 Sep 8.30–7.45; Oct 9.30–5.30; Nov–Easter 9.30–5 (closed 9–27 Jan)
♿ Poor: narrow access to elevator
💰 Expensive

HIGHLIGHTS

● The main exhibition hall and stairway
● The view over the Basin of St. Mark from the Punta della Dogana
● The Torrino

TIPS

● Allow time to enjoy the building as well as the art.
● There's an excellent bookshop and pleasant café/bar within the complex.

Venice's most exciting contemporary space, wonderfully positioned where the Canal Grande opens into St. Mark's Basin, showcases cutting-edge, 21st-century art in a converted 17th-century building.

The history The buildings of the Dogana di Mare, Venice's historic customs house, stand at the tip of Dorsoduro, the Punta della Dogana, where the Giudecca Canal merges with the Canal Grande. These warehouses, culminating in a tower and portico, were designed by Giuseppe Benoni and built between 1677 and 1682. Neglected for years, in 2007 the buildings were leased by the city to François Pinhault, owner of the Palazzo Grassi (▷ 70). In June 2009, after a €20 million restoration, the 3,440sq m (37,000sq ft) space opened as

Far left: Maurizio Cattelan's Untitled 2007; *middle: the* Boy with a Frog *sculpture by Charles Ray stands outside the galleries and alongside the Canal Grande; below: Punta della Dogana at dusk*

a permanent contemporary art museum, its interior transformed by Japanese minimalist architect Tadao Ando. Inspired by traditional vernacular architecture, the interior fuses the old brick and stone with steel, glass and concrete.

The galleries Pinhault's personal vision and taste dictate much of what's on show—an evolving display that he views as an ongoing project, featuring works from his collection, commissioned pieces from up-and-coming artists, and important temporary exhibitions. Among the former, works by Richard Prince, Rachel Whiteread, Jeff Koons and Cindy Sherman have been on show. The violence inherent in some contemporary work is disturbing, but the Punta della Dogana has brought a new vibrancy to the Venetian art scene.

THE BASICS

palazzograssi.it

➕ H7

✉ Campo di Salute, Dorsoduro 2

☎ 041 240 1308

🕐 Daily 10–7

🍴 Museum café serving snacks and light meals

🚤 Salute

♿ Good

💰 Expensive

HIGHLIGHTS

● The Ponte di Rialto
● The Pescheria
● The produce stalls

TIP

● Remember the fish market is closed on Monday and there are no markets on Sunday.

The Ponte di Rialto, one of Venice's most iconic sights, spans the Canal Grande to link the *sestiere* of San Marco with the Rialto, once the city's commercial hub and still home to the main food markets.

The Ponte di Rialto The *rivo alto*, the "high bank," was one of the firmest areas of the lagoon, so it's no surprise that the first settlements of Venice grew up here, the district becoming the commercial heart of the city. The two banks were linked by a pontoon bridge and the first permanent wooden structure went up in the 13th century. Merchants traded European goods with exotic imports from the East, while international banks and trading companies influenced prices across the known world. This monopoly ceased in 1498, when

Clockwise from far left: The beautiful Ponte di Rialto; a stall in the fish market on the Rialto; looking across the bridge towards Campo San Bartolomeo; the bridge lit at night

Vasco da Gama rounded the Cape and opened up sea routes to India and the Far East. The present bridge (1588–91) was designed by Antonio da Ponte, who won the commission in a competition, beating architects Palladio and Sansovino. The shops are later additions.

The markets The Rialto is still a trading center, though today the accent is on food, with the open areas crammed with fish, fruit and vegetable stalls. The surrounding streets, whose evocative names recall the commodities traded here, house some of the city's best grocers, butchers, bakers, dairy shops and delicatessens. There's no better way to appreciate Venice as a living city than to join the morning shoppers and enjoy the sights, scents and sounds of one of Europe's most colorful markets.

THE BASICS

🔸 H4–H5
✉ Ponte di Rialto
🕐 Market Mon–Sat
8–12.30; fish market
closed Mon
🍴 Bars in and around the
food markets
🚊 Rialto Mercato 1,
Rialto 1, 2
♿ Poor
🎟 Free

HIGHLIGHTS

- Facade (1559–80)
- Lighthouses (1828)
- Campanile (1791)
- *Adoration of the Shepherds*, Jacopo Bassano
- *The Fall of Manna*, Tintoretto
- *The Last Supper*, Tintoretto
- Choir
- View from the campanile

If asked, many Venetians would probably nominate the view from the bell tower of San Giorgio Maggiore, a magnificent Palladian church on its own island near the Giudecca, as the city's finest.

Classical The church's dazzling marble facade provides one of the great panoramic set pieces of the Venetian skyline. Originally founded in 790, the first church on the site was destroyed by an earthquake in 1223, together with an adjoining Benedictine monastery built in 982 and donated to the order by the doge.

While the monastery was rebuilt in 1443, the church had to wait over a hundred years until 1559 and the arrival of the great Vicenzan architect, Andrea Palladio. His design for the new church adopted many of the architectural

Left: A gondola passes in front of the church of San Giorgio Maggiore, with its bell tower to the left of the picture; below: The view from the bell tower across the lagoon

idioms of the ancient world (notably the majestic four-column portico) to produce one of Italy's most beautiful neoclassical buildings.

Interior The ancient world also influenced the sparse interior, where light is introduced by high windows, a device borrowed from the bathhouses of third-century Rome. The major works of art are Jacopo Bassano's *Adoration of the Shepherds* (1582), above the second altar on the right, and a pair of outstanding paintings by Tintoretto—*The Fall of Manna* (1594) and *The Last Supper* (1594)—on the walls of the chancel. Behind the high altar is the choir (1594–98), with its impressive wooden stalls, and down a corridor off the north aisle is the elevator up the campanile. The trip to San Giorgio is worth it for the views alone.

THE BASICS

🔒 K8
✉ Campo San Giorgio, Isola di San Giorgio Maggiore
☎ 041 522 7827
🕐 Apr–Oct daily 9–7; Nov–Mar 8.30–6
🍴 Giudecca
🚤 San Giorgio N, 2
♿ Poor
🔔 Campanile moderate

PAVLO CALIARIO VERONEN PICTORI
NATV°Æ AMVLO ARTIS MIRACVLO
SV ERST VE FAT°S FAMA VICTVRO

HIGHLIGHTS

● Sacristy
● Ceiling
● Choir and nuns' choir
● Organ
● *St. Nicholas* (1563), Titian (first chapel on right)
● *Madonna and Child* (16th century), Tommaso Lombardo (second chapel on right)
● *Tomb of Archbishop Podocattaro of Cyprus* (d.1555), Sansovino (fourth chapel on right)

While paintings by some of Venice's artists—notably Titian and Tintoretto—are often showcased in grandiose settings, the city's finest collection of works by Veronese is in the humble little church of San Sebastiano.

Veronese Born in Verona, Paolo Caliari Veronese (1528–88) moved to Venice while he was in his twenties, settling close to San Sebastiano, which became his parish church. In 1555 he was commissioned to decorate the sacristy, where he left paintings of the *Evangelists* and the *Coronation of the Virgin*. Impressed by his work, the church authorities gave him free rein to decorate the ceiling. The three main panels depict episodes from the story of Esther, chosen for its symbolic parallels with the stories of Eve and the Virgin Mary.

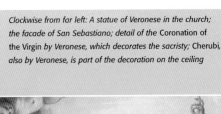

Clockwise from far left: A statue of Veronese in the church; the facade of San Sebastiano; detail of the Coronation of the Virgin by Veronese, which decorates the sacristy; Cherubi, also by Veronese, is part of the decoration on the ceiling

Monopoly Veronese also painted the high altarpiece—the *Madonna and Child with Saints Sebastian, Peter, Francis and Catherine* (1570)—and the two vast paintings on the north and south walls. The latter portray *Saints Mark and Marcellinus Led to Martyrdom and Comforted by St. Sebastian* and *The Second Martyrdom of St. Sebastian* (Sebastian survived his first assault by arrows and was martyred by being pummelled to death). Veronese also painted *The Trial and Martyrdom of St. Sebastian* in the nuns' choir, above the church's west end. He even designed and painted the organ.

His decorative monopoly of San Sebastiano makes it only fitting that he was buried here. His tomb, and that of his brother, lie in front of the chapel.

THE BASICS

chorusvenezia.org
🔲 D7
✉ Campo San Sebastiano, Dorsoduro 1686
☎ 041 275 0462
🕐 Mon 10.30–4, Tue–Sat 10.30–4.30
🍴 Campo Santa Margherita and Campo San Barnaba
🚤 San Basilio N, 2, 6, 8
♿ Good
💶 Inexpensive
❓ Chorus Pass and City Pass (▷ 4)

HIGHLIGHTS

● Facade bas-reliefs (1440), Antonio Gambello
● Upper facade, Mauro Coducci
● *Madonna and Child with Saints*, Giovanni Bellini
● Relics of San Zaccaria
● *The Birth of John the Baptist*, Tintoretto
● Crypt
● Vault frescoes, Andrea del Castagno
● Altarpieces, Antonio Vivarini and Giovanni d'Alemagna
● Predella, Paolo Veneziano

San Zaccaria is a charming medley of Gothic and Renaissance architecture. Its calm interior contains Giovanni Bellini's *Madonna and Child with Saints*, one of Venice's most beautiful altarpieces.

Changes San Zaccaria was founded in the ninth century, received a Romanesque veneer a century later, and was overhauled once more in 1174. Rebuilding began again in the 14th century, when the church acquired a Gothic look, though no sooner had it been completed than another new church was begun. Old and new versions are still visible, the brick facade of the earlier church on the right, the white marble front of the latter to its left. The newer facade is one of the most important in Venice, displaying a moment of architectural transition from

Clockwise from far left: The restored Madonna and Child with Saints by Giovanni Bellini (1505); the church was built in the 15th century and completed by Mauro Coducci; the bell tower; the lower facade is Gothic and the upper part Renaissance in style; marble carvings on the ceiling

Gothic to Renaissance. The Gothic lower half is by Antonio Gambello, while the Renaissance upper section (added after Gambello's death in 1481) is the work of Mauro Coducci.

Who's who? The nave's second altar contains Giovanni Bellini's *Madonna and Child with Saints* (1505). Across the nave in the second altar on the right lie the relics of San Zaccaria (Zachary), father of John the Baptist. The "museum" off the south aisle has linked chapels; the first has an early Tintoretto, *The Birth of John the Baptist*. The vaults of the adjoining Cappella di San Tarasio have early Renaissance frescoes by Andrea del Castagno and Gothic altarpieces by Antonio Vivarini. Steps lead to a ninth-century crypt, resting place of eight doges.

THE BASICS

✚ K6
✉ Campo di San Zaccaria, Castello 4693
☎ 041 522 1257
🕐 Mon–Sat 10–12, 4–6, Sun 4–6
🍴 Campo San Provolo
🚢 All services to San Zaccaria
♿ Good
💶 Church free. Cappella di San Tarasio inexpensive

HIGHLIGHTS

- Facades
- Martial bas-reliefs
- Plaque recording 1916 incendiary bomb
- Campanile's stone mask
- Interior
- *Madonna della Misericordia*, Bartolomeo Vivarini
- *Santa Barbara*, Palma il Vecchio

Santa Maria Formosa's appeal rests partly in its surrounding square. An archetypal Venetian *campo*, it is a pleasantly rambling affair, full of local vibrancy and lined with attractive cafés and palaces.

The structure This church takes its name from *una Madonna formosa*, "a buxom Madonna," which appeared to St. Magnus in the seventh century, instructing him to follow a small white cloud and build a church wherever it settled. The present building, completed in 1492, was grafted onto an 11th-century Byzantine church, from which it borrowed its Greek-cross plan, a common feature of Byzantine (and later) churches dedicated to the Virgin. The facade (1542) was paid for by the Cappello family, hence its statue of Vincenzo Cappello, a

Left: Santa Barbara by Palma il Vecchio depicts her flanked by other saints; below: Santa Maria Formosa was built onto an earlier Byzantine church

Venetian admiral. Note the carved face on the bell tower to the left, one of Venice's most famous grotesques.

Interior The church's interior is a unique blend of Renaissance decoration and ersatz Byzantine cupolas, barrel vaults and narrow-columned screens. Of particular interest are two paintings, the first being Bartolomeo Vivarini's *Madonna della Misericordia* (1473), a triptych in the first chapel on the right (south) side. It was financed by the church's congregation which is depicted in the picture sheltering beneath the Virgin's protective cloak. The second and more famous picture, Palma il Vecchio's *Santa Barbara* (1522–24), depicts the patron saint of artillerymen, and portrays the artist's daughter as its model.

HIGHLIGHTS

- *Madonna and Child*, Giovanni Bellini
- *Assumption*, Titian
- *Madonna di Ca' Pesaro*, Titian
- *Madonna and Child* (1339), Paolo Veneziano (sacristy)
- *St. John the Baptist*, Donatello
- *Mausoleo Tiziano* (Tomb of Titian)
- Wooden choir (124 stalls)
- *Monumento al Doge Giovanni Pesaro*
- *Monumento al Canova*

If you were allowed to walk away with just one work of art from Venice it could well be Bellini's sublime altarpiece in this church, the largest and most important in the city.

Magnificent edifice The Frari narrowly outranks Santi Giovanni e Paolo in size and importance. Founded around 1250, it became the mother church of the city's Franciscans, after whom it is named—*frari* is a Venetian corruption of *frati*, meaning "friars."

The greats interred Many of the city's great and good are buried in the church, among them the painter Titian (d.1576), whose 19th-century tomb occupies the second altar on the right (south) wall. Opposite, on the left wall, stands the *Monumento al Canova*

Far top left: A triptych (1488) by Giovanni Bellini, depicting the Madonna and Child with saints and angels; far bottom left: The tomb of Doge Francesco Dandelo; middle: Carved wooden inlaid stalls in the Gothic-Renaissance choir; below: A statue by Jacopo Negretti

(1827), an unmistakable marble pyramid that contains the sculptor's heart. The composer Claudio Monteverdi (d.1643) is buried in the third chapel to the left of the high altar.

Art Titian's compelling and stylistically innovative *Assumption* (1516–18) above the high altar immediately draws your eye, and don't miss the same artist's influential *Madonna di Ca' Pesaro* (1526), near the north door. The church's most beautiful painting, however, is Giovanni Bellini's sublime triptych of the *Madonna and Child between Sts. Nicholas, Peter, Mark and Benedict* (1488), in the sacristy. In the first chapel on the right of the high altar you will find Donatello's statue of *St. John the Baptist* (1438), the only work in Venice by the famous Florentine sculptor.

THE BASICS

chorusvenezia.org

🚇 E5

✉ Campo dei Frari 3072, San Polo 3072

☎ 041 275 0462

🕐 Mon–Sat 9–6, Sun 1–6. Last admittance 5.30

🍴 Campo dei Frari

🚏 San Tomà N, 1, 2

♿ Good: one or two steps

💷 Inexpensive

❓ Chorus Pass (▷ 4)

HIGHLIGHTS

- Tinted marbles
- Decorative inlays
- False pillars
- Bas-reliefs
- Nuns' choir
- Balustrade
- Pillar carving
- Raised choir
- *Madonna and Child*, Nicolò de Pietro
- Ceiling

You'll soon get used to being brought up short in Venice by surprises and views around almost every corner, but none of them quite compares with your first glimpse of the beautiful marbles of Santa Maria dei Miracoli.

Miracles The church was built to house an image of the Virgin, painted in 1409 and originally intended to be placed on the outside of a house (a common practice in Venice). Miracles *(miracoli)* began to be associated with the image in 1480, leading to a flood of votive donations that enabled the authorities to commission a church for the icon from Pietro Lombardo. One of the leading architects of his day, Lombardo created a building that relied for its effect almost entirely on shades,

Left: The unusual interior makes use of marble and is decorated with statues by the architect Pietro Lombardo and his sons; below: Lombardo also used marble to great effect on the exterior of the church

hues and tints, facing his church in a variety of honey-toned marbles, porphyry panels and serpentine inlays.

Interior grandeur Lombardo's innovative use of marble continues on the inside, which is filled with an array of sculptures that were executed in tandem with his sons, Tullio and Antonio. The best include the carving on the two pillars that support the nuns' choir (near the entrance); on the half-figures of the balustrade fronting the raised choir; and among the exotica at the base of the choir's pillars. The striking ceiling portrays *50 Saints and Prophets* (1528), by Pier Pennacchi and his assistants. Nicolò di Pietro's *Madonna and Child*, the miraculous image for which the church was built, adorns the high altar.

THE BASICS

chorusvenezia.org

🔢 J4

✉ Campo dei Miracoli, Cannaregio 6075

☎ 041 275 0462

🕐 Mon 10.30–4, Tue–Sat 10.30–4.30

🍴 Campo Santa Maria Nova

🚤 Rialto N, 1, 2

♿ Good

💶 Inexpensive

❓ Chorus Pass and City Pass (▷ 4)

HIGHLIGHTS

- Marble floor
- *Descent of the Holy Spirit*, Titian
- *The Virgin Casting out the Plague*, Juste le Court
- *Feast at Cana* (1561), Tintoretto (sacristy)
- *Cain and Abel* (1542–44), Titian (sacristy)
- *David and Goliath* (1542–44), Titian (sacristy)
- *Sacrifice of Abraham* (1542–44), Titian (sacristy)
- *St. Mark Enthroned between Sts. Cosmas, Damian, Roch and Sebastian* (1510), Titian (sacristy)

In a city where almost every street and canal offers a memorable vista, this church, proudly situated at the entrance to the Canal Grande, forms part of the famous panorama most people commonly associate with Venice.

Plague In 1630 Venice found itself ravaged by an outbreak of the plague so devastating that the Senate promised to build a church in celebration of the Virgin if she could save the city. Within weeks the pestilence had abated and, on 1 April the following year, the first stone of the Salute, meaning "health" and "salvation" in Italian, was laid. Its architect was Baldassare Longhena.

His design proved to be a baroque model for years to come, combining the Palladian

Clockwise from far left: Santa Maria della Salute has been listed as a World Heritage Site by UNESCO; the church seen from gondolas and other passenger craft; the interior of the dome; a view of a circular detail and statue on the exterior

influence of his master, Vincenzo Scamozzi (Andrea Palladio's closest follower), with a range of personal innovations.

Baroque interior The Salute's main impact is as a distant prospect, its dazzling exterior detail and great dome (fashioned on St. Peter's in Rome) forming irreplaceable elements of the Venetian skyline. The interior is more restrained, and its fine marble floor first catches the eye. Moving left from the side entrance, the third of the three altars has an early work by Titian, the *Descent of the Holy Spirit* (1550). The high altar supports *The Virgin Casting out the Plague* (1670), a sculpture designed by Longhena and carved by Juste le Court. The supplicant figure represents Venice, while the elderly harridan moving off right symbolizes the plague.

THE BASICS

✚ G7

✉ Campo della Salute, Dorsoduro

☎ 041 241 1018 or 041 274 3928

🕐 Daily 9–12, 3–5.30

🚤 Salute 1

♿ Poor: several steps

⛪ Church free. Sacristy inexpensive

HIGHLIGHTS

- Main portal
- *Monument to Doge Pietro Mocenigo*, Pietro Lombardo
- *St. Vincent Ferrer*, Giovanni Bellini
- *St. Antonius Pierozzi Giving Alms to the Poor*, Lorenzo Lotto
- *Monument to Doge Michele Morosini*
- Veronese ceiling paintings, Cappella del Rosario
- Capella della Madonna della Pace

Nowhere in Venice is there a greater collection of superb sculpture under one roof than in this majestic Gothic church. The walls here are lined with the funerary monuments of more than 20 of the city's important doges.

Monuments Santi Giovanni e Paolo, known locally as San Zanipolo, is rivaled only by Santa Maria Gloriosa dei Frari (▷ 48–49). Its appeal rests on a handful of superb paintings, its tremendous tombs, and on surroundings that include the magnificent facade of the adjacent Scuola Grande di San Marco and Verrocchio's great equestrian statue of Bartolomeo Colleoni. The church was begun in 1246 by Doge Giacomo Tiepolo, who is buried in the most ornate of the four wall tombs built into the

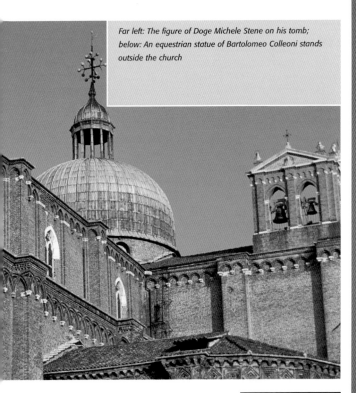

Far left: The figure of Doge Michele Stene on his tomb; below: An equestrian statue of Bartolomeo Colleoni stands outside the church

facade. Inside, further tombs lie around the walls, many by some of Venice's finest medieval sculptors. The best include the monuments to Doge Pietro Mocenigo (d.1476) by Pietro, Tullio and Antonio Lombardo (left of the main door), and to Doge Michele Morosini (d.1382), on the wall to the right of the high altar.

Paintings The most outstanding of the church's paintings are Giovanni Bellini's beautiful and recently restored polyptych of St. Vincent Ferrer (1464, second altar on the right) and the works in the south transept, which include *The Coronation of the Virgin*, attributed to Cima da Conegliano, and Lorenzo Lotto's wonderful *St. Antonius Pierozzi Giving Alms to the Poor* (1542).

THE BASICS

basilicasantigiovannie
paolo.it

➕ J4

✉ Campo Santi Giovanni e Paolo, Castello 6363

☎ 041 523 5913

🕐 Mon–Sat 9–6, Sun 12–6.30

🍴 Campo Santi Giovanni e Paolo

🚢 Fondamente Nove or Ospedale 4.1, 4.2, 5.1, 5.2

♿ Good: one step

💶 Inexpensive

HIGHLIGHTS

- Facade
- Stucco staircase
- Ceiling paintings
- Albergo and Archivio
- *Judith and Holofernes*, Piazzetta
- *St. Nicholas of Bari*, Lorenzo Lotto
- *Nativity*, Cima da Conegliano

Giovanni Battista Tiepolo's paintings are not to all tastes, but those in the intimate Scuola Grande dei Carmini, all pastel shades and fleshy figures, are a change from the drama of Titian or Tintoretto.

Carmelites The Carmelite Order's Venetian chapter was originally installed in Santa Maria del Carmelo (or dei Carmini), the Carmelite church just to the left of the *scuola* (▷ right). In 1667 the order commissioned Baldassare Longhena to design a new home in the present building (Longhena also designed Santa Maria della Salute and a number of palaces on the Canal Grande).

Exuberant ceilings The highlights are Giovanni Battista Tiepolo's nine ceiling paintings

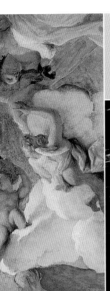

Left: Flight of Angels *by Sebastiano Ricci; below: The Sala dell'Archivio*

(1739–44) in the Salone. The paintings' central panel depicts the vision of St. Simon Stock, elected the Carmelites' prior-general in 1247, in which the Virgin appears to the saint with a "scapular." This garment of two linked pieces of cloth became central to Carmelite belief as wearers were promised relief from the pains of purgatory on the "first Sunday after death." Two adjacent rooms, the Albergo and Archivio, have heavy wooden ceilings and several paintings, the best of which is Piazzetta's *Judith and Holofernes* (1743).

Chiesa dei Carmini Be sure to visit the church to see Lorenzo Lotto's *St. Nicholas of Bari* (1529), by the side door (second chapel), and Cima da Conegliano's fine *Nativity* (1509) above the second altar on the (south) wall.

THE BASICS

➕ D6
✉ Campo dei Carmini, Campo Santa Margherita, Dorsoduro 2617
☎ 041 528 9420
🕐 Daily 11–5
🍴 Campo Santa Margherita
🚤 Ca' Rezzonico 1
♿ Poor: stairs to main rooms
💶 Moderate

Chiesa dei Carmini
🕐 Mon–Sat 2.30–5.30
💶 Free

HIGHLIGHTS

- *Crucifixion*
- *Moses Strikes Water from the Rock*
- *The Fall of Manna*
- *The Temptation of Christ*
- *The Adoration of the Shepherds*
- *Wooden sculptures*
- *The Flight into Egypt*
- *Annunciation*

TIPS

- Allow 1 to 2 hours for a thorough visit.
- Start your visit upstairs in the Albergo.

In a city of superlative and striking works of art, there can be few that make such a marked and powerful first impression as the colossal cycle of 54 paintings by Tintoretto that line the walls here.

From rags to riches This *scuola*, formerly a charitable institution for the sick, was founded in 1478 in praise of St. Roch, whose efficacy against disease made him very popular in pestilence-ridden Venice. In 1564, as one of wealthiest fraternities, the *scuola* instigated a competition to decorate its hall. The winner, Tintoretto, spent some 23 years creating one of Europe's greatest painting cycles.

The wonders inside To see Tintoretto's 54 paintings in the order they were painted, ignore

Clockwise from far left: Detail of the Crucifixion (1565), one of a series of 54 paintings by Tintoretto; the Annunciation, also by Tintoretto; the exterior of the building; the heavily decorated Upper Great Hall in the scuola

the canvases on the ground level and in the main hall (Sala Grande) up the stairs. Instead, go to the Sala dell'Albergo (off the main hall), dominated by a huge *Crucifixion* (1565), often described as one of Italy's greatest paintings. The room's central ceiling panel is *St. Roch in Glory*, the painting that won Tintoretto his commission. In the main hall are ceiling paintings (1575–81) describing episodes from the Old Testament, all carefully chosen to draw parallels with the *scuola*'s charitable or curative aims. The 10 wall paintings show scenes from the New Testament. Note the superb 17th-century wooden carvings around the walls, by the little-known sculptor Francesco Pianta. Of the eight paintings downstairs, the artist's last in the *scuola* (1583–88), the best are the idiosyncratic *Annunciation* and *The Flight into Egypt*.

THE BASICS

scuolagrandesanrocco.it

⊞ E5

✉ Campo San Rocco, San Polo 3052

☎ 041 523 4864

🕐 Daily 9.30–5.30

🍴 Campo dei Frari

🚤 San Tomà N, 1, 2

♿ Poor

💰 Expensive

❓ A leaflet about the *scuola*'s paintings is usually free with your ticket; audio guides are also available

24 Scuola di San Giorgio degli Schiavoni

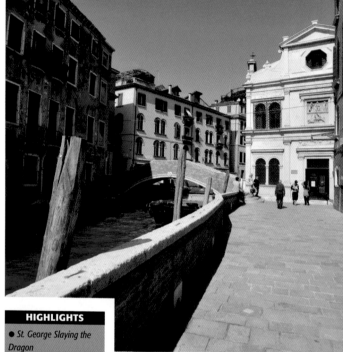

HIGHLIGHTS

● St. George Slaying the Dragon
● Triumph of St. George
● St. George Baptizing the Gentiles
● The Miracle of St. Tryphon
● The Agony in the Garden
● The Calling of St. Matthew
● The Vision of St. Augustine

TIP

● Allow time for your eyes to accustom to the dim light, and take time to pick out the detail in the paintings.

This intimate *scuola,* with its charming Carpaccio paintings, allows you the opportunity to look at works of art in the building for which they were painted, rather than in a gallery venue.

Slavs This tiny *scuola* (religious or charitable confraternity) was founded in 1451 to look after Venice's Dalmatian, or Slav *(Schiavoni),* population. Dalmatia, roughly present-day Croatia, was among the first of the territories absorbed by Venice (in the ninth century). In 1502 Vittore Carpaccio, famous for his St. Ursula cycle in the Gallerie dell'Accademia, was commissioned to decorate their humble *scuola* with scenes illustrating the lives of Dalmatia's three patron saints: St. George, St. Tryphon and St. Jerome. On their completion (in 1508), the

Clockwise from left: Looking towards the scuola; detail of St. George Slaying the Dragon by Carpaccio; stone fish detail on the exterior

paintings was installed in the headquarters' upper gallery and later moved to their present position when the *scuola* was rebuilt in 1551.

Art cycle The nine-painting cycle starts on the north wall with *St. George Slaying the Dragon* (1502–08), while to its right is the *Triumph of St. George*, *St. George Baptizing the Gentiles* and *The Miracle of St. Tryphon*, which depicts the boy-saint exorcizing a demon from the Roman Emperor's daughter. Right of the altarpiece by Carpaccio's son, Benedetto, are *The Agony in the Garden* and *The Calling of St. Matthew*, followed by three works featuring St. Jerome, an early church father. The best known is the *Vision of St. Augustine*, with the saint in his study having a vision announcing Jerome's death.

K5

Calle dei Furlani, Castello 3259/a

041 522 8828

Mon 2.45–6, Tue–Sat 9.15–1, 2.45–6, Sun 9.15–1

Fondamenta di San Lorenzo

All services to San Zaccaria

Good

Moderate

61

● Basilica di Santa Maria Assunta
● Santa Fosca church
● View from the campanile

The rural backwater of Torcello, in the far northeast of the lagoon, is Venice's most ancient settlement. It's the site of a superb basilica, the oldest building in Venice.

Seeing Torcello From the landing stage a path runs beside Torcello's canal, crossed by the simple stone span of the Ponte del Diavolo (Devil's Bridge), to the main piazza. Grouped around here is everything there is to see. You will also find the so-called Trono di Attila, a primitive stone chair once used by the bishop.

Island churches One of the most magical places in Venice, Torcello was probably the city's birthplace and the first area of the lagoon settled in the fifth century. Malaria and the silting up of its canals snuffed out its prosperity

Clockwise from far left: The view from the bell tower across Torcello; candles inside Santa Fosca church; Madonna and child mosaic in Santa Maria Assunta; exterior of Santa Fosca; a canal runs through farmland; a mosaic depicting hell in Santa Maria Assunta

in the 12th century, and today it is home to little more than a single hamlet and a beautiful patchwork of green fields and leafy canals. Torcello is dominated by the cathedral of Santa Maria Assunta. This is Venice's oldest building (founded 639) and one of its loveliest sights as well as the finest Veneto-Byzantine church in Italy. The lofty interior, bare and cool, has some superb mosaics dating from the ninth to 12th centuries, on the vaults and walls. Climb the bell tower for wonderful lagoon views across the mudflats and marsh. Also worth seeing close by are the 11th-century Byzantine church of Santa Fosca and the small Museo dell'Estuario, which houses a low-key display of archaeological finds from Torcello and the lagoon. The perfect antidote to the crowds and heat of Venice.

THE BASICS

➕ See map ▷ 115
🚢 Line 12 from Fondamente Nove to Burano, then No. 9 boat to Torcello, every 60–90 min, takes 45 min. Get the earliest boat to avoid a crowd

Museo dell'Estuario
☎ 041 730 119
🕐 Mar–Oct daily 10.30–5.30; Nov–Feb 10–5
🎟 Inexpensive

Basilica di Santa Maria Assunta
☎ 041 730119
🕐 Mar–Oct daily 10.30–6; Nov–Mar 10–5
❓ Bell tower temporarily closed
🎟 Church and bell tower inexpensive. Moderate for combined ticket

More to See

This section contains other great places to visit if you have more time. Some are in the heart of the city while others are a short journey away, found under Farther Afield. This chapter also has fantastic excursions that you should set aside a whole day to visit.

In the Heart of the City

ANGELO RAFFAELE

The ancient church of the Archangel Raphael was founded in the eighth century; the present Greek cross-shaped building, with its two bell towers, dates from the 17th. Well off the beaten track, its visitor numbers soared following the success of Salley Vickers' book *Miss Garnet's Angel*; the church plays a starring role in the novel. Above the main door stands a charming statue of the Angel, holding the hand of the boy Tobias, accompanied by a dog, and holding a fish, which plays a key role in the story. Inside, there are more reminders of the apocryphal story, with the stars of the show painted on the organ loft by Gianantonio Guardi.

C6 Campo Angelo Raffaele, Dorsoduro 1721 Daily 9–12, 3–5 San Basilio 2, 8 Free

ARSENALE

The Arsenale, Venice's vast former shipyards, are now used for exhibitions during Venice's *Biennale* and for the annual Festival of Boats each May. Work on opening more areas, more frequently, is ongoing with a view to reinstating the entire area as a vibrant part of the city.

M6 Campiello della Malvasia, Castello 041 270 9546 1, 4.1, 4.2 Varies with exhibition

CA' PESARO

capesaro.visitmuve.it

The Ca' Pesaro presents its best face to the Canal Grande, but its waterfront facade can also be glimpsed from the ends of several alleys off the Strada Nova. It was bought as three separate buildings in 1628 by the Pesaro family, who subsequently commissioned Baldassare Longhena, one of Venice's leading 17th-century architects, to unite the component parts behind one of the city's grandest baroque facades. Today it houses Venice's Galleria d'Arte, Galleria Internazionale d'Arte Moderna (Gallery of Modern Art) and the Museo d'Arte Orientale displaying Chinese and Japanese art and objects.

Beautiful Ca' Pesaro houses galleries of modern and oriental art

G4 ✉ Canal Grande-Fondamenta
Ca' Pesaro, Santa Croce 2070–76 ☎ 041
721127 🕐 Galleria and Museo Apr–Oct
Tue–Sun 10–6; Nov–Mar 10–5 🚤 San Stae
N, 1 ♿ Poor 💰 Galleria and Museo
expensive

CAMPO DEI MORI

This sleepy little square may take
its name either from the Moorish
merchants who traded on the
fondaco nearby, or from three silk
merchants—Robia, Sandi and Alfani
Mastelli who settled in the Palazzo
Mastelli north of the *campo*. In
time they may have inspired the
so-called *Mori* (Moors), three
statues built into the walls of the
piazza's houses. The building
stands just east of the square at
No. 3399 and was home to the
painter Tintoretto between 1574
and his death in 1594.

G2 ✉ Campo dei Mori, Cannaregio
🚤 Orto 4.1, 4.2, 5.1, 5.2

CAMPO SANTA MARGHERITA

This may well become your
favorite Venetian square, thanks
mainly to its friendly and informal
air, its collection of little bars and
cafés, and its easy-going street life,
which remind you that Venice is
still a living city. It's busy with
Venetians throughout the day,
shopping at the market stalls in the
morning, meeting to chat and sip
coffee in the afternoons while
children play and dogs race round.
Evenings see flocks of students
from the nearby university drinking
outside bars; Margaret Duchamp,
on the corner, Il Caffè and Il Doge
are all popular and have outside
tables. The Scuola Grande di San
Rocco (▷ 58), the Frari (▷ 48),
and the Accademia (▷ 24) are
within easy reach.

E6 ✉ Dorsoduro 🍴 Cafés
🚤 Ca' Rezzonico 1

GESUITI

This lofty, shadowy and incredibly
ornate church, built by the Jesuits
in 1715, is renowned for its
extraordinary marble *trompe-l'œil*,
best seen in the pulpit on the left,
whose solid stone is carved to
resemble pelmets, tassels and
curtains of figured damask and

Informal Campo Santa Margherita

Tintoretto's house in Campo dei Mori

velvet. The church also boasts Titian's *Martyrdom of St. Lawrence* (in the first chapel on the left) and Tintoretto's *Assumption of the Virgin* (in the left transept).

⊞ J3 ⊠ Campo dei Gesuiti, Cannaregio 4885 ☎ 041 523 1616 ◷ Daily 10–12, 4–6/7 🚢 Fondamente Nove 4.1, 4.2, 5.1, 5.2 ♿ Good 💵 Free

IL GHETTO

The Venetian ghetto lies in a fascinating area half-hidden in a corner of Cannaregio, enclosed by canals. The city's Jewish population were forced to live here until 1527. The district, which gave its name to all similar enclaves, most likely took its name from the foundries where cannon were cast (*gettare* means to cast). The area is still one rich in Jewish culture and history, including a monument to the city's Jews murdered during the Holocaust, synagogues and the Jewish museum, the Museo Ebraico.

⊞ E2

Museum

⊠ Campo Ghetto Nuovo, Cannaregio 2902 ☎ 041 715 359; museoebraico.it

◷ Jun–Sep Sun–Fri 10–7; Oct–May 10–5.30 🚢 Guglie 4.1, 4.2, 5.1, 5.2 or San Marcuola N, 1, 2 💵 Moderate

GIARDINI SAVORGNAN

Push open the iron gate on the Fondamenta Savorgnan on the Canale di Cannaregio and discover one of the area's best-kept secrets, the surprisingly spacious, tree-shaded Giardini Savorgan. Once the private garden of the *palazzo* standing on one side, this grassy space is a great place for a picnic or a breather.

⊞ E3 ⊠ Fondamenta Savorgnan, Cannaregio 3012 🚢 Guglie 4.1, 4.2, 5.1, 5.2 💵 Free

GIARDINO PAPADOPOLI

The Giardino Papadopoli, once one of the largest private gardens in Venice, stands at the west end of the Canal Grande, a stone's throw from bustling Piazzale Roma. It's a great place to wait for transportation to the mainland, by road or rail—you can reach the station across the Ponte della Costituzione, opened in 2007 to

Colorful apartment buildings in Il Ghetto

Tulips blooming in Giardino Papadopoli

mark the new millennium. The gardens were laid out in 1810 when a group of buildings were demolished, including the church of Santa Croce, which gave its name to this *sestiere*.

➕ D4 ✉ Fondamenta Papadopoli
🚏 Piazzale Roma 1, 2 💶 Free

ISOLA DI SAN MICHELE

It's a short hop on the *vaporetto* to Venice's atmospheric cemetery island with its Renaissance church. Most of Isola di San Michele is covered by the cemetery, where Venetians are buried in tiers of stone coffin drawers or rest under an assortment of monuments. Don't miss the tombs of the composer Stravinsky and the impresario Serge Diaghilev.

➕ L1–L2 ✉ Isola di San Michele
☎ 041 729 2811 🕐 Apr–Sep daily 7.30–6; Oct–Mar 7.30–4; 25 Dec, 1 Jan 7.30–12
🚏 Cimitero 💶 Free

MERCERIE

The *calli* between San Marco and Rialto are known as the Mercerie, once synonymous with luxury goods. Today, the shops sell everything from expensive high fashion to tourist kitsch.

➕ H5 🚏 Rialto N, 1, 2, 4

MUSEO DELLA FONDAZIONE QUERINI STAMPALIA

querinistampalia.it
The Fondazione Querini Stampalia, housed in a Renaissance *palazzo*, promotes study and culture. Its modernized ground floor is an excellent example of the work of architect Carlo Scarpa. The museum is in the unchanged period rooms on the second floor, giving a real taste of an 18th-century *palazzo*. Stars of the show are Giovanni Bellini's superb *Presentation in the Temple* and two series of paintings: 67 studies of Venetian festivals by the 18th-century artist Gabriele Bella, and a collection of genre paintings by Pietro Longhi (1702–85) showing everyday Venetian life.

➕ J5 ✉ Campiello Querini Stampalia, Castello 5252 ☎ 041 271 1411
🕐 Tue–Sun 10–6 🚏 San Zaccaria, 1, 2, 4.2, 5.2 💶 Expensive

The cemetery on Isola di San Michele

The Geography Lesson by Pietro Longhi in Museo della Fondazione Querini Stampalia

MUSEO STORICO NAVALE

The enjoyably presented displays of maritime ephemera here put Venice and the sea into a clear historical context.

⊞ M7 ⊠ Campo San Biagio, Castello 2148 ☎ 041 244 1399 ◉ Mon–Fri 8.45–1.30, Sat 8.45–1 🚢 Arsenale 1, 4.1, 4.2 ♿ Poor 💰 Inexpensive

PALAZZO CONTARINI DEL BOVOLO

scalacontarinidelbovolo.com

This Gothic *palazzo* is best known for its sinuous exterior staircase. Such staircases are called *scale a chiocciola* (snail stairs) in Italian—the Venetian dialect for snail is *bovolo*. The beautiful redbrick and Istrian stone stairway gives access on five levels to graceful loggias curving around inside a tower.

⊞ G6 ⊠ Calle dei Risi, San Marco ◉ Tue–Sun 10.30–1.30, 2–6 🚢 Rialto N, 1, 2 ♿ None 💰 Moderate

PALAZZO GRASSI

palazzograssi.it

Outside, nothing could be more traditionally 18th-century classical than this palace. Inside, it's another story; the interior was converted in the 1980s by Gianni Agnelli of Fiat to become Venice's most high-profile exhibition venue. In 2004, following the death of Agnelli, it was bought by François Pinault, the French millionaire collector and owner of a business empire that includes Gucci. It reopened in 2007 as a venue for temporary exhibitions, designed to be seen in conjunction with the collection at the Punta della Dogana (▷ 36–37) and centered round Pinhault's own collection of more than 2,000 pieces of 20th- and 21st-century contemporary art.

⊞ F6 ⊠ Campo San Samuele, San Marco 3231 ☎ 199 139 139 (in Italy), 00 39 0445 230313 (from abroad) ◉ Wed–Mon 10–7 🚢 Sant'Angelo 1, San Samuele 2 💰 Expensive

PALAZZO MOCENIGO

mocenigo.visitmuve.it

The Palazzo Mocenigo near San Stae is one of several *palazzi* in the city built by the Mocenigo family, one of the grandest and oldest

Museo Storico Navale

Palazzo Contarini del Bovolo with its famous exterior staircase

of the noble Venetian clans. The palace now houses the Museo del Tessuto e Costume and is worth a visit for a fascinating glimpse of the style in which the 18th-century nobility lived.

➕ F4 ✉ Salizzada San Stae, Santa Croce 1992 ☎ 041 721 798 🕐 Tue–Sun 10–4 🚤 San Stae N, 1 🚻 Moderate

PONTE DELL'ACCADEMIA

All the bridges across the Canal Grande have mesmerizing views, but none perhaps as lovely as those looking east from the Ponte dell'Accademia. There's been a bridge here since 1854; today's is the third version. It's identical in design to the Ponte degli Scalzi at the station, but built of wood, as stone was too expensive for construction across this much wider stretch of water.

➕ F7 ✉ Canal Grande 🚤 Accademia N, 1, 2 ♿ Poor

RIVA DEGLI SCHIAVONI

This broad quayside with its procession of *palazzi*, historic hotels, stalls and cafés, has great views, and is an ideal place for an evening stroll.

➕ K6–L6 ✉ Riva degli Schiavoni, San Marco to Castello 🚤 All services to San Zaccaria

SAN FRANCESCO DELLA VIGNA

San Francesco takes its name from a vineyard left to the Franciscans here in 1253. Many alterations have been made since, not least the facade, built by Palladio between 1562 and 1572. The best paintings are Antonio da Negroponte's *Madonna and Child* (1450), in the right transept, and Giovanni Bellini's *Madonna and Child* in the Cappella Santa, from where you can access the cloisters.

➕ L5 ✉ Campo San Francesco, Castello 2786 ☎ 041 523 5341 🕐 Daily 8–12, 3–7 🚤 Celestia 4.1, 4.2, 5.1, 5.2 ♿ Good 🚻 Free

SAN GIACOMO DELL'ORIO

chorusvenezia.org

Few Venetian buildings feel as old as San Giacomo, founded in the ninth century and added

Riva degli Schiavoni

Interior decoration at San Francesco della Vigna

to over the years to produce an architectural hybrid. The 14th-century Gothic ship's-keel ceiling and the wooden Tuscan statue of the *Madonna and Child* are wonderful. There are superb paintings in the old and new sacristies and a high altarpiece, *Madonna and Child*, by Lorenzo Lotto.

F4 ⊠ Campo San Giacomo dell'Orio, Santa Croce 1456 ☎ 041 275 0462; chorusvenezia.org ● Mon 10.30–4, Tue–Sat 10.30–4.30 ⛴ Riva di Biasio or San Stae 1 ♿ Good ⟐ Inexpensive ❓ Chorus Pass and City Pass (➤ 4)

SAN GIOVANNI IN BRAGORA

Many people have a soft spot for San Giovanni in Bragora, the baptismal church of the Venetian composer Antonio Vivaldi.

Founded in the eighth century, it is one of Venice's oldest churches, its name deriving possibly from *brágora*, meaning "market-place," or from two dialect words, *brago* ("mud") and *gora* ("stagnant canal"); or from the Greek *agora*, meaning "town square"; from *bragolare* ("to fish"); or from the region in the Middle East that yielded the relics of St. John the Baptist, to whom the church is dedicated. The Venetian composer Antonio Vivaldi was baptized here, and the original font, together with copies of his baptismal documents, are in the left nave.

The paintings in the lovely interior begin on the south wall to the left of the first chapel with a triptych by Francesco Bissolo and a *Madonna and Saints* by Bartolomeo Vivarini. Between these, above the confessional, stands a small Byzantine Madonna. A relief above the sacristy door is flanked on the left by Alvise Vivarini's *Risen Christ* (1498) and by Cima da Conegliano's *Constantine and St. Helena* (1502). Cima also painted the church's pictorial highlight, *The Baptism of Christ* (1494). On the wall of the left aisle is a small *Head of the Saviour* by Alvise Vivarini and Bartolomeo Vivarini's *Virgin Mary between John the Baptist and St. Andrew* (1478), to the right of the second chapel.

The attractive interior of the church of San Giovanni in Bragora

L6 ✉ Campo Bandiera e Moro, Castello 3790 ☎ 041 724 1044 🕐 Mon–Sat 9–12 🏛 Campo Bandiera e Moro 🚌 All services to San Zaccaria 🚻 Good 💶 Free

SAN MAURIZIO

artemusicavenezia.it

Rebuilt in the early 19th century and hardly used in the 20th, the church of San Maurizio found a new role in 2004 when it opened as a Vivaldi exhibition area. The chief draw is the fine collection of old musical instruments, whose sound provides the music that's a constant backdrop to your visit. You can buy CDs and DVDs relating to the composer.

G6 ✉ Campo San Maurizio, San Marco ☎ 041 241 1840 🕐 Daily 10–7 🚌 Giglio 1 💶 Free

SAN NICOLÒ DEI MENDICOLI

San Nicolò was built in the 12th century and since 1966 it has been restored by the Venice in Peril Fund. The interior is superbly decorated with marbles, statues, panels, paintings and gilded woodwork.

C6 ✉ Campo San Nicolò dei Mendicoli, Dorsoduro 1907 ☎ 041 270 2464 🕐 Mon–Sat 10–12, 4–6 🚌 San Basilio N, 2, 6, 8 🚻 Good 💶 Free

SAN PANTALEONE

San Pantaleone is best known for its gargantuan ceiling painting, Gian Antonio Fumiani's *The Miracles and Martyrdom of St. Pantaleone* (1704). Smaller paintings include Veronese's touching piece *St. Pantaleone Healing a Boy* (1587; second chapel on the right).

E5 ✉ Campo San Pantalon, San Polo 3765 ☎ 041 270 2464 🕐 Mon–Sat 3–6 🚌 San Tomà 1, 2 🚻 Good 💶 Free

SAN POLO

Founded in 837 but much altered since, the church of San Polo is renowned for Giandomenico Tiepolo's *Via Crucis*, or *Stations of the Cross* (1747), an 18-panel cycle of paintings in the sacristy. Tintoretto's turbulent *Last Supper* (1547) hangs on the west wall, while the apse chapel contains Veronese's *Marriage of the Virgin*.

The view along a street to San Pantaleone

An exhibition in San Maurizio

🔢 F5 ✉️ Campo San Polo, San Polo 2102
☎️ 041 275 0462; chorusvenezia.org
🕐 Mon 10.30–4, Tue–Sat 10.30–4.30
🚤 San Silvestro 1 ♿ Good
💷 Inexpensive ❓ Chorus Pass and City
Pass (▷ 4)

SANTO STEFANO

Delight in the sensation of walking from the bustle of the city into a building that induces immediate calm, an effect gained by the soothing Gothic interior of this, one of Venice's loveliest churches. Ideally placed Santo Stefano sits on the edge of Campo Santo Stefano (also known as Campo Francesco Morosini), one of Venice's most charming squares; the nearby Paolin (▷ 150) is an ideal place to sit with a drink or ice cream.

The church has not always been so peaceful. It was reconsecrated six times to wash away the stain of blood spilled by murders within its walls. Today, its interior is over-arched by an exquisite ship's keel ceiling and framed by tie beams and pillars of Greek and red Veronese marble. In the middle of the nave lies Doge Francesco Morosini (d.1612, and buried under Venice's largest tomb slab). He was famous for recapturing the Peloponnese and blowing up the Parthenon with a single shot.

Other tombs, notably Pietro Lombardo's *Monument to Giacomo Surian* (d.1493) on the wall to the right of the main door, command attention, but the church's chief artistic interest lies in the gloomy sacristy at the end of the right nave. The altar wall displays two narrow-framed saints by Bartolomeo Vivarini, as well as a recessed 13th-century Byzantine icon. On the walls to either side are four paintings by Tintoretto and four portraits of Augustinian cardinals, displayed here as Santo Stefano is an Augustinian church.

🔢 G6 ✉️ Campo Santo Stefano (Campo Francesco Morosini), San Marco 2774
☎️ 041 275 0462; chorusvenezia.org
🕐 Mon 10.30–4, Tue–Sat 10.30–4.30
🍴 Campo Santo Stefano 🚤 San Samuele or Sant' Angelo N, 1, 2 ♿ Very good
💷 Inexpensive ❓ Chorus Pass and City
Pass (▷ 4)

The leaning bell tower of Santo Stefano is a tourist attraction

SQUERO DI SAN TROVASO

Venice had more than 10,000 gondolas in the 16th century; today there are only a few hundred, built in a handful of specialist boatyards *(squeri)*. One of the most famous, and easiest to see, is the Squero di San Trovaso, on the waterfront of the Rio San Trovaso, just behind the Zattere. Construction sheds and workshops are set back from the *rio*, and there's generally activity of some sort as gondolas are repaired. Modern water conditions take a toll on the boats, which suffer from the backwash of motorboats, and they need to be cleaned and overhauled as often as once a month. To get a real insight into the expertise of the gondolier, take a *traghetto* across the Canal Grande and watch the oarsmen.

➕ E7 ✉ Rio San Trovaso, Dorsoduro 🚤 Zattere N, 2, 5.1, 6, 8, 10

TEATRO LA FENICE

teatrolafenice.it

Fenice is the Italian for phoenix, and Venice's opera house, designed by Giannantonio Selva in 1792, rose from the ashes of the disastrous fire of 1996 to reopen for the 2004–5 season. The new hall is a delight. You should book well in advance for performances or join one of the regular tours.

➕ G6 ✉ Campo San Fantin, San Marco 1965 ☎ 041 786672 🕐 Daily with audio guides to fit around rehearsals; check with theater. For group guided tours tel 041 786675; festfenice.com 🚤 Giglio 1 💲 Expensive

TORRE DELL'OROLOGIO

torreorologio.visitmuve.it

San Marco's clock tower was built between 1496 and 1506. The exterior stone dial shows the 24 hours in Roman numerals; the interior face shows the signs of the zodiac and phases of the moon.

➕ J6 ✉ Piazza San Marco, San Marco 30124 ☎ Book online or tel 848 082 000 (from abroad 00 39 041 4273 0892); reservations compulsory 🕐 Guided visits in English Mon–Wed 10, 11, Thu–Sun 2, 3 🚤 San Marco Vallaresso, San Marco Giardinetti N, 1, 2 and all services to San Zaccaria 💲 Expensive

The auditorium, Teatro La Fenice

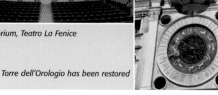

Torre dell'Orologio has been restored

Farther Afield

BURANO

Tucked into the northeast of the lagoon, Burano combines its role as a functioning fishing community with that of a tourist honeypot. Its streets and canals are lined with brightly colored houses, making it an impossibly picturesque draw. It has always been noted for its lace making, and you can see superb examples at the Museo del Merletto, though much of the lace on sale in the souvenir shops is imported from the far east.

➕ a4–c5   ✉ Isola di Burano   🚢 12 from Fondamente Nove, every 60–90 min

Museo del Merletto

➕ b5   ✉ Piazza Galuppi 187   ☎ 041 730 034   🕐 Apr–Oct Tue–Sun 10–6; Nov–Mar Tue–Sun 10–5   💶 Moderate

THE LIDO

The Lido is essentially a long, narrow sandbank, once a sparsely inhabited island of dunes and pine-woods. Today it combines its role as a residential suburb with that of a seaside resort and overspill hotel area for Venice. A 10-minute boat trip from the city will bring you to a different world, where cars, buses and supermarkets are the backdrop to lazy beach days. More active pursuits include tennis and golf, as well as walking and cycling. You could also take in some of the Lido's superb art nouveau and art deco buildings, such as the Hotel Excelsior, a neo-Moorish fantasy.

➕ See map ▷ 115   🚢 Lido

SANT'ERASMO

Bigger than Venice itself, Sant'Erasmo is one of the lagoon's best-kept secrets. It lies northeast of the city, a long, flat, sparsely inhabited island where sandy paths crisscross well-kept fields and tiny vineyards. Sant'Erasmo produces huge quantities of vegetables for the city markets. The island is traversed by a single road, where rickety old unlicensed cars trundle up and down. The island does have a tiny store at the main settlement, built around the church, and a couple of *trattorie*.

➕ See map ▷ 115   ✉ Isola di Sant' Erasmo   🚢 Capannone, Chiesa, Punta Vela 13 from Fondamente Nove

A quiet canal on Burano at dawn with moored vessels and colorful houses

Excursions

CHIOGGIA

turismovenezia.it/chioggia

This excursion takes in the west end of the Lido and the island of Pellestrina en route to the ancient town of Chioggia.

Pellestrina is a contrast to the developed, bustling Lido, a sand-swept spit of land, bordered on the sea side by the *murazzi*, the sea defence walls erected in the 18th century. Its three main villages earn their living from fishing, both from the boats you'll see moored and from the floating huts just offshore.

Chioggia is a Roman foundation and one of the earliest settlements on the lagoon, a past reflected in its layout, a grid pattern of three straight streets intersected by canals. The main street, Corso del Popolo, is lined with old buildings and is home to the 14th-century *granaio* (grainstore), behind which is the *pescheria*, the fish market. Further along the Corso are the churches of Sant'Andrea Apostolo, San Jacopo and the Duomo (cathedral).

Past here, the Museo Civico della Laguna Sud is housed in a 15th-century Franciscan convent. It tells the story of Chioggia and the southern lagoon, with displays on the Roman epoch and a collection of boats and fishing artifacts on the upper floors.

From here, head east along the main Canale della Vena, an almost impossibly picturesque waterway with brightly painted fishing boats, tiny arcaded shops, fruit and vegetable stalls and flapping washing in the adjoining court-yards. The waterfront is the main food shopping street and thronged all morning, while the narrow *calli* leading off illustrate how the town has retained its medieval layout.

The church of San Domenico, standing on its own island at the lagoon end, was founded in the 13th century and contains the 1520 *St. Paul,* the last picture painted by Carpaccio.

Do try to include lunch while in Chioggia; the restaurants here are noted for their fish and seafood, and prices are lower than in Venice. You could stop on the way back to town for a swim at one of Pellestrina's quiet beaches or at the Lido itself.

Distance: From the Lido 25km (16 miles)
Journey time: 1 hour from the Lido
Transport: Co-ordinated bus and waterbus service; No. 11 bus from Lido, connect with *motonave* 11 to Chioggia from Pellestrina

Museo Civico della Laguna del Sud

✉ San Francesco Fuori le Mure, Campo Marconi, Chioggia ☎ 041 550 0911 🕐 Jun–Aug Tue–Wed 9–1, Thu–Sun 9–1, 9–11; Sep–May Tue–Sun 9–1 💶 Moderate

Bridge over the Canale della Vena

PADUA

turismopadova.it

Historic Padua is a university city and important economic center, where art, monuments, churches and shops are scattered around a compact, attractive center. Aim to arrive early, taking the tram from outside the station to the center.

The historic hub centers around the Palazzo della Ragione, medieval Padua's assembly hall and law courts, built from 1218 to 1219. The vast building has a remarkable cycle of 15th-century astrological frescoes in the main hall, which also contains a huge wooden horse, constructed for a tournament in 1466. The ground floor has been home to food stalls for more than 800 years, while the Piazza della Frutta and Piazza dell'Erbe, on each side of the *palazzo*, host one of northern Italy's most vibrant produce markets.

Near here is the splendidly eclectic Caffè Pedrocchi, whose upstairs rooms, the 19th-century center of Padovan intellectual life, are decorated in every style from Egyptian and Etruscan to Renaissance. South of here, reached down Via del Santo, is the Basilica di Sant'Antonio, one of Italy's main pilgrim shrines, built between the mid-13th and 14th centuries and flanked by a superb equestrian bronze of Gattamelata by Donatello (1453).

Padua's main artistic site lies to the north, nearer the station, a complex including the Cappella degli Scrovegni, the Musei Civici Eremitani and the Palazzo Zuckermann. The Scrovegni chapel was built in 1300 by Enrico Scrovegni to atone for his father's usury. From 1303 to1309 the walls were frescoed by Giotto with scenes from the life of Christ and the Virgin, set against a radiant blue background. Considered one of the turning points in Western art, the perspectival elements, the realistic details and expressions show a wholly innovative naturalism and fluency. The other parts of the complex showcase archaeology, sculpture, painting and the decorative and applied fine arts.

Distance: 32km (20 miles)
Journey time: 25–35 min
Transport: Bologna line from Venezia Santa Lucia; GSITA buses from Piazzale Roma
🚉 Stazione FS ☎ 049 201 0080
🕐 Mon–Sat 9–7, Sun 10–4
🚉 Galleria Pedrocchi ☎ 049 201 0080
🕐 Mon–Sat 9–6

Cappella degli Scrovegni

cappelladegliscrovegni.it
✉ Piazza Eremitani 8 ☎ 049 201 0020;
book by phone or online 72 hours in advance, tickets to be collected 1 hour in advance 🕐 Daily 9–7 💶 Expensive

Outside Basilica di Sant'Antonio

VICENZA

vicenzae.org

Cradled in green hills, beautiful Vicenza, with its glossy shops, smart restaurants and easy lifestyle, is famed for its *palazzi* and civic buildings, the work of the 16th-century's most influential architect, the great Andrea Palladio.

Dating from Roman times, the town stands on two rivers and became a Venetian possession in 1404. Its architectural makeover came in the 16th century when Palladio and his neoclassical style burst upon the scene. Born in Padua, Palladio found his major patron, the humanist Trissino, in Vicenza and, between 1540 and 1580, transformed the city.

Vicenza is bisected by the Corso Palladio, lined with a procession of mansions and *palazzi*, no fewer than five designed by Palladio, while others are scattered throughout the city center. The Corso opens into Piazza Matteotti, home to both the Teatro Olimpico and the Palazzo Chiericati (1550), one of Palladio's most triumphant buildings, now housing the Museo Civico and its fine art collection. Teatro Olimpico, Europe's oldest indoor theater, was designed by Palladio in 1579 and opened in 1585. The architect died before it was complete, though the astonishing *trompe l'oeil* permanent stage set of a classical city was inspired by his designs.

South from here lies the Piazza dei Signori, the heart of the *centro storico*. The square is dominated by Palladio's Basilica, enclosing the earlier Gothic Palazzo della Ragione, and his Loggia del Capitaniato, flanked by the Monte di Pietà, Vicenza's 16th-century pawn shop.

Elsewhere you'll find the Palazzo Leoni Montanari, home to another museum, the Duomo (cathedral) and some interesting churches.

Outside Vicenza are two renowned Palladian villas, Villa Valmarana, nicknamed "Ai Nani" after the stone dwarfs on its wall, with superb frescoes by Tiepolo father and son, and Villa Capra Valmarana, or Rotonda (1567).

Distance: 74km (47 miles)
Journey time: 55 min
Transport: Trains from Venezia Santa Lucia
🛈 Piazza Matteotti 12 ☎ 0444 994770
🕐 Daily 9–5.30

Teatro Olimpico
✉ Piazza Matteotti 11, 36100 Vicenza
☎ 0444 964 380 🕐 Sep–Jun Tue–Sun 9–5; Jul–Aug 9–6 💷 Expensive (combined ticket for all Vicenza sites)

Museo Civico–Pinacoteca
✉ Palazzo Chiericati, Piazza Matteotti 37–39
☎ 0444 222 811 🕐 Sep–Jun Tue–Sun 9–5; Jul–Aug 10–6 💷 Expensive (combined ticket)

An ariel view across Vicenza

City Tours

This section contains self-guided tours that will help you explore the sights in each of the city's regions. Each tour is designed to take a day, with a map pinpointing the recommended places along the way. There is a quick reference guide at the end of each tour, listing everything you need in that region, so you know exactly what's close by.

CITY TOURS

San Marco

The historic *sestiere* of San Marco, the true heart of the city, is packed with *palazzi,* churches, museums, shops and restaurants. It runs east of the Canal Grande, from the iconic Piazza San Marco west towards the Rialto and its famous bridge.

Morning

Start your day in the **Piazza San Marco** (▷ 34–35; right), visiting the rich interior of the basilica before the hordes of day-visitors from the cruise boats and coaches arrive. Then take the elevator up the **Campanile** (▷ 34–35), from where you'll get a bird's-eye view of the city, its lagoon and the islands, the perfect way to get your Venetian bearings.

Mid-morning

Splash out on mid-morning coffee at one of the piazza's celebrated cafés, before you stroll across to the **Palazzo Ducale** (▷ 32–33). Here, in the vast and opulent chambers, you'll get an insight into the grandeur and riches of Venice at the height of its power. If you want to learn more, spend an hour in the **Museo Correr** (▷ 30–31) at the opposite end of the piazza.

Lunch

There's a huge choice of lunch possibilities between the piazza and the **Rialto** (▷ 38–39)—a good bet would be **Acquapazza** (▷ 144), where you can sit outside and enjoy the freshest of fish on Campo Sant'Angelo, one of the area's nicest *campi.*

Afternoon

Spend the afternoon wandering through the maze of streets and squares towards the Rialto and its bridge, perhaps visiting the **Teatro La Fenice** (▷ 75), taking in some contemporary art at **Palazzo Grassi** (▷ 70; left), or the lovely **Santo Stefano** (▷ 74). If you're flagging, use the *vaporetti* along the Canal Grande.

Mid-afternoon

It's time to browse the shops of San Marco, where you'll find everything from the cheapest souvenirs to serious *alta moda* (high fashion). Good areas to shop are along the **Mercerie** (▷ 69), around Campo San Bartolomeo at the **Rialto** (▷ 38–39; right), or go where the serious money spends its cash and head for Calle Vallaresso, around the church of San Moïse and along the Largo XXII Marzo, an area that's home to just about every top Italian designer you can name. There are plenty of souvenir stalls on the waterfront near San Marco, some selling sketches, prints and watercolors.

Evening

Aim to finish your stroll on Campo Santo Stefano, where you can have a drink or one of the best ice creams in town at **Paolin** (▷ 150).

Dinner

Have dinner away from the piazza itself, but return later to see this wonderful space thronged with people and buzzing with conversation; not for nothing did Napoleon call it the "finest drawing room in Europe." Pull up a chair, listen to the music and sip a glass of Prosecco at **Caffè Florian** (▷ 147; left) or another of the piazza cafés.

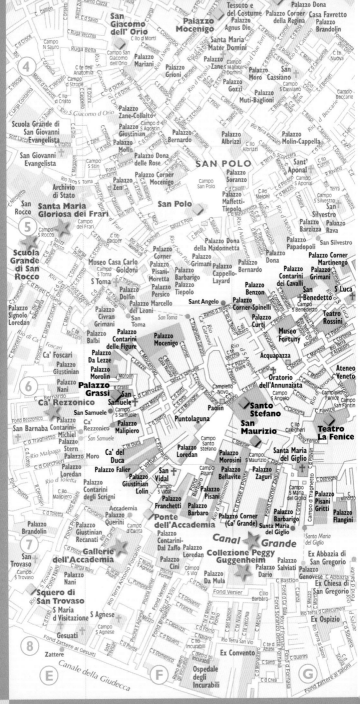

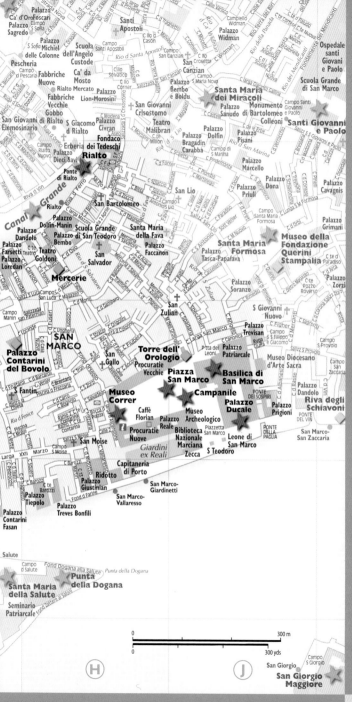

Palazzo Ca' d'OroFoscari
Palazzo Campo
Sagredo S Sofia
S Sofia Michiel
delle Colonne
Pescheria
Fabbriche
Nuove
Ca' da Mosto
Rialto Mercato Palazzo Lion-Morosini
Fabbriche Vecchie
Gobbo
San Giovanni di Rialto
Elemosinario
Palazzo Civran
Erberia dei Tedeschi
Rialto
Ponte di Rialto
Riva del Vin
Canal Grande
Rialto
Palazzo Dolfin-Manin
Palazzo Dandolo
Palazzo Farsetti
Palazzo Loredan
Scuola Grande di San Teodoro
Palazzo Bembo
Teatro Goldoni
San Salvador
Santa Maria della Fava
Palazzo Faccanon
Mercerie
SAN MARCO
Palazzo Contarini del Bovolo
S Fantin
Rio di Fenice
Torre dell' Orologio
Procuratie Vecchie
Museo Correr
Caffè Florian
Procuratie Nuove
Palazzo Reale
Piazza San Marco
Basilica di San Marco
Campanile
Palazzo Ducale
Museo Archeologico
Biblioteca Nazionale Marciana
Zecca
Leone di San Marco
Piazzetta San Marco
S Teodoro
Giardini ex Reali
Capitaneria di Porto
San Marco-Giardinetti
Ridotto
Palazzo Giustinian
San Marco-Vallaresso
Palazzo Tiepolo
Palazzo Treves Bonfili
Palazzo Contarini Fasan

Santi Apostoli
Palazzo Widman
Ospedale santi Giovanni e Paolo
Scuola dell'Angelo Custode
San Canzian
Palazzo Bembo e Boldu
Santa Maria dei Miracoli
Monumento di Bartolomeo
Santa Maria Nova
San Giovanni Crisostomo
Teatro Malibran
Palazzo Bragadin Carabba
Palazzo Dolfin
Palazzo Pisani
Palazzo Marcello
Colleoni
Scuola Grande di San Marco
Santi Giovanni e Paolo
Palazzo Dona
Palazzo Priuli
San Lio
Palazzo Cavagnis
Palazzo Grimani
Santa Maria Formosa
Museo della Fondazione Querini Stampalia
Palazzo Tasca-Papafava
Palazzo Soranzo
Palazzo Zorzi
San Giovanni Nuovo
Palazzo Trevisan
Palazzo Patriarcale
Museo Diocesano d'Arte Sacra
Palazzo Dandolo
Riva degli Schiavoni
Palazzo Prigioni
PONTE DEI SOSPIRI
PONTE DELLA PAGLIA
PONTE DEL VIN
San Marco-San Zaccaria

Salute
Campo d Salute
Fond Dogana alla Salute
Punta della Dogana
Santa Maria della Salute
Seminario Patriarcale

0   300 m
0   300 yds

(H)   (J)   San Giorgio
Campo S Giorgio
San Giorgio Maggiore

San Marco Quick Reference Guide

Basilica di San Marco (▷ 14)
A superb 1,000-year-old church, rich in mosaics, whose architecture looks both to ancient Byzantium and medieval Europe. The treasures inside the building match its striking interior. The altar is encrusted with precious gems.

Museo Correr (▷ 30)
Venice's city museum, telling the story of the historic Republic through sculpture, paintings, maps and artifacts. The paintings here represent Venice's finest artists. A hall is dedicated to sculptures by Antonio Canova.

Palazzo Ducale (▷ 32)
Once the seat of government and home to the Doge, this extraordinary palace is unique architecturally and artistically. Here you will find the largest oil painting in the world, by Tintoretto. The Bridge of Sighs is nearby.

Piazza San Marco and Campanile (▷ 34)
Venice's greatest square, lined with splendid buildings and arcades, is dominated by the detached Campanile with its views over the city and lagoon, and in fine weather to the Alps.

Rialto (▷ 38)
Once the commercial hub of the city, the Rialto bridge spans the Canal Grande, attracting locals and tourists to browse its wonderfully colorful fresh produce markets. Nearby streets house food shops.

CITY TOURS

Cannaregio

Venice's northwest *sestiere*, Cannaregio, one of the earliest areas to be developed, was, before the causeway and railway were built, the original entrance to the city. Full of contrasts, it sprawls from the station to the Rialto along the Canal Grande, an area that's busy and still densely populated by local Venetians. To the north, things are quieter, and you'll find peaceful residential streets running between the wide *fondamente* (quaysides) that line a trio of parallel canals lying to the south of the open waters of the lagoon.

Morning

The **Canal Grande** (▷ 20–21) is at its most animated in the mornings, when it's bustling with *vaporetti*, delivery barges and flotillas of gondola tours. There are few better places to take in all this activity than from the portico of the upper floor of the **Ca' d'Oro** (▷ 16–17; right), so kick off your day by visiting this beautiful *palazzo* and its museum.

Mid-morning

You'll emerge to turn left on to the **Strada Nova**, a string of wide streets which connects the Rialto with the station and was created in the 19th century when numerous old houses were demolished. There's plenty of choice for a coffee break and the area is known for its good-value and wide range of shops. Turn right when you get to the Canale di Cannaregio and cut through to visit **Il Ghetto** (▷ 68). From here, head north, following the *fondamenta* along one of Cannaregio's wide canals.

Lunch

There's a choice of lunch spots along these canals; you could enjoy some *cichetti* (Venetian-style tapas) or a full lunch at **Anice Stellato** (▷ 145; left) or take your time at the **Osteria l'Orto dei Mori** (▷ 149–150).

Afternoon

After lunch, cut through the **Campo dei Mori** (▷ 67) to visit the lovely church of **Madonna dell' Orto** (▷ 26–27; right). Then either walk or hop on the *vaporetto* to the Fondamenta Nuove, to take in the over-the-top delights of the sumptuous church of the **Gesuiti** (▷ 67–68).

Mid-afternoon

Follow the maze of streets south to **Santa Maria dei Miracoli** (▷ 50–51; left), one of Venice's loveliest churches and a popular spot for weddings.

Evening

Enjoy a drink at an outside table, either in **Campo Santa Maria Nova**, right near the Miracoli and one of Venice's most under-rated squares, or at a café in **Santi Apostoli**, always busy with locals and visitors.

Dinner

This part of Cannaregio has a good choice of restaurants and you couldn't do better than head for **Vini da Gigio** (▷ 151), which belongs to an association of restaurants that prides itself on serving genuine Venetian cuisine, with the accent on seasonal, fresh, traditional dishes. If you're up for more action, you could round off the evening by dropping in to Venice's **Casino** (▷ 135), housed in the magnificent Palazzo Vendramin Calergi, right on the Canal Grande.

Canale delle Sacche

Canale delle Navi

1

Ex Ospedale
Psichiatrico
Umberto I

Sant'Alvise

Rio d Riformati
Fond d Riformati

Rio di Sensa

C llo
Cavallo

Ospedale
Fatebenefratelli

Le Cappuccine
Palazzo
Grimani Mayer
Fond d Cappuccine
Rio di Cappuccine
Rio di San Girolamo
Fond San Girolamo

Palazzo
Michiel

Sant'Alvise
Convento

C llo
Plave

Scuola
dei Mercanti

S Girolamo

Rio d Ormesini
Fond d Ormesini
Rio di Misericordia

Anice
Stellato

Rio di Sensa

Fond Madonna dell'orto
Rio Madonna dell'orto

Palazzo
Mastelli

CANNAREGIO

Campo
Ghetto
Nuovo

**Campo
del Mori**

2

**IL
GHETTO**

Museo
Ebraico

Osteria l'Orto
dei Mori
Palazzo
Longo

Casa
Tintoretto

Palazzo
Nani

Tempio
Israelitico

Ex Convento
dei Servi di Maria

Canale di Cannaregio
Fond Savorgnan

Campo
S Leonardo

Rio Terra S Leonardo

Cappella del
Volto Santo

Palazzo
Savorgnan

Palazzo
Venier

**Giardini
Savorgnan**

Guglie

Fond Canal

Palazzo
Diedo

Campo
S Marziale

3

PONTE
D EUGLIE

Ex Chiesa
di San Leonardo

Ex Scuola
di Cristo

Rio Terra di Maddalena

La Maddalena

Palazzo
Correr
Contarini

Palazzo
Labia

Palazzo
Emo

San
Marcuola

Palazzo Vendramin-
Calergi (Casino)

Palazzo Correr
Contarini

S Fosca

Campo
S Geremia

**San Geremia
e Lucia**

Palazzo
Correr
Contarini

Palazzo
Gritti

Campo
Marcuola

San Marcuola
Casino

Palazzo
Soranzo
Emo

Palazzo
Molin

Riva di
Biasio

Palazzo
Marcello
Toderini

Palazzo
Giovanelli

Canal

Palazzo
Barbarigo

Palazzo
Flangini

Fondaco
dei Turchi

Palazzo
Belloni
Battagia

Grande

Palazzo
Corner

Palazzo
Gidoni-
Bembo

Casa
Corner

Museo
di Storia
Naturale

Ca'
Tron

Palazzo
Priuli-
Bon

San Stae

Palazzo Gussoni-
Grimani della Vida

Palazzo
Gritti

Palazzo
Dona-
Balbi

San Giovanni
Decollato

Palazzo
Priuli-Stazio

Campo
S Stae

Palazzo
Boldu

Campo
S Simeon
Grande

**S Simeon
Grande**

Palazzo
Foscarini-
Giovanelli

4

**San
Giacomo
dell' Orio**

**Palazzo
Mocenigo**

Museo del
Tessuto e
del Costume

Ca' Pesaro

Palazzo Dona

Palazzo
Soranzo
Cappello

Ruga Bella

Campo
N Sauro

Palazzo
Mariani

Campo S
Giacomo
dell'Orio

Palazzo
Grioni

Santa Maria
Mater Domini

Palazzo Corner
della Regina

Casa
Favretto

Palazzo Agnus Dio

Palazzo
Zane

San
Cassiano

Palazzo
Brandolin

Palazzo
Moro

Campo
S Cassiano

Palazzo
Gozzi

Palazzo
Muti-Baglioni

5

San Giovanni
Evangelista

Scuola Grande di
San Giovanni
Evangelista

Palazzo
Zane-Collalto

Palazzo
Giustinian

Palazzo
Bernardo

Palazzo
Albrizzi

Palazzo
Molin-Cappella

Sant'
Aponal

Palazzo
Molin

Palazzo Dona
delle Rose

SAN POLO

Campo
S Aponal

Archivio
di Stato

E

Palazzo Corner
Mocenigo

Palazzo
Zen

San Polo

Campo
San Polo

F

Palazzo
Soranzo

Palazzo
Maffeti-Tiepolo

G

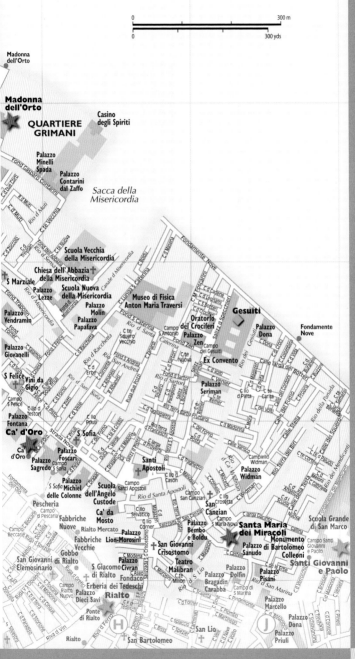

0   300 m

0   300 yds

Madonna
dell'Orto

**Madonna
dell'Orto**

Casino
degli Spiriti

**QUARTIERE
GRIMANI**

Palazzo
Minelli
Spada

Palazzo
Contarini
dal Zaffo

*Sacca della
Misericordia*

Scuola Vecchia
della Misericordia

Chiesa dell'Abbazia
della Misericordia

S Marziale

Palazzo
Lezze

Scuola Nuova
della Misericordia

Palazzo
Molin

Museo di Fisica
Anton Maria Traversi

Palazzo
Vendramin

Palazzo
Papafava

Oratorio
dei Crociferi

Gesuiti

Palazzo
Zen

Palazzo
Dona

Fondamente
Nove

Palazzo
Giovanelli

Campo
dei Gesuiti

S Felice   Vini da
Gigio

Ex Convento

Campo
S Felice

Palazzo
Seriman

Palazzo
Fontana

Ca' d'Oro

Ca'
d'Oro

Palazzo
Foscari

S Sofia

Palazzo
Sagredo

Campo
S Sofia

Santi
Apostoli

Palazzo
Widman

Pescheria

Palazzo
Michiel
delle Colonne

Scuola
dell'Angelo
Custode

Campo
Santi Apostoli

Rio di Santa Apostoli

Campo
d'Pescaria

Fabbriche
Nuove

Ca' da
Mosto

San
Canzian

Campo
San Canzian

Scuola Grande
di San Marco

Rialto Mercato

Campo
S Maria Nova

Fabbriche
Vecchie

Lion-Morosini

Palazzo

Gobbo

Palazzo
Bembo
e Boldu

**Santa Maria
dei Miracoli**

San Giovanni di
Elemosinario

S Giacomo
di Rialto

San Giovanni
Crisostomo

Fondaco

Teatro
Malibran

Palazzo di
Sanudo

Bartolomeo

**Santi Giovanni
e Paolo**

Palazzo
Civran

Monumento
Colleoni

Campo
Giovanni
e Paolo

Erberia dei Tedeschi

Campo
Rialto
Nuovo

Palazzo
Dieci Savi

Palazzo
Bragadin
Carabba

Palazzo
Dolfin

Palazzo
Pisani

Rialto

Ponte
di Rialto

Campo di
Marina

Palazzo
Marcello

Rialto

San Bartolomeo

San Lio

Palazzo
Dona

Palazzo
Priuli

SIGNTS AND EXPERIENCES

Ca' d'Oro (▷ 16)

The Ca' d'Oro, set right on the Canal Grande and one of Venice's finest Venetian-Byzantine *palazzi*, is a perfect example of a rich medieval merchant's home and place of business. It was built between 1420 and 1434 for the Contarini family and gets its name —the House of Gold—from the glittering decoration that once adorned the exterior. Today, it houses an eclectic museum.

Madonna dell'Orto (▷ 26)

This gem of a church, set in a quiet and undiscovered area on Venice's northern fringes, was founded in 1350 and rebuilt in the Gothic style between 1399 and 1473. The facade combines Gothic and Renaissance elements, while the interior is pure, airy Gothic. The superb paintings are almost all by Tintoretto, who lived nearby and is buried here. He created these works as a gift to the church.

Santa Maria dei Miracoli (▷ 50)

This perfectly proportioned and balanced Renaissance church, set alongside a canal, was built in the 1480s in honor of a miraculous shrine to the Virgin that stood nearby. The exterior is faced with polychrome marble panels, columns and pilasters, best admired from the bridge. Inside, the light-filled space has intricate and delicate carving and sculptures.

Restaurant tables set out in Campo Santa Maria Nova

Castello

Castello, the biggest Venetian *sestiere*, stretches from San Marco in the west to encompass the islands of San Pietro and Sant'Elena in the east. Historically, its shipbuilding Arsenale was the city's industrial heart, still surrounded by a vibrant working-class district. Its cityscape is varied, with a long southern waterfront, the Riva degli Schiavoni, overlooking St. Mark's Basin and a northern quayside that looks towards the main lagoon islands and the distant Alps.

CITY TOURS

Morning
Head first for **Campo Santa Maria Formosa**, where you can visit the church (▷ 46–47; right) and take in the art collection at the **Museo della Fondazione Querini Stampalia** (▷ 69) before exploring the surrounding *calli*, busy at this time of day with locals shopping. From here, head up to **Santi Giovanni e Paolo** (▷ 54–55) and its *campo*, now home to Venice's main hospital, housed behind the superb facade of what was once the Scuola Grande di San Marco.

Mid-morning
Emerging from the church, take a pause to enjoy a drink at one of the cafés surrounding the *campo*, before using your map to wend your way through the labyrinthine alleys to the serene Palladian church of **San Francesco della Vigna** (▷ 71). From here follow the crowds southeast towards the **Arsenale** (▷ 66), a short hop from the **Museo Storico Navale** (▷ 70) where you can learn more about Venice's maritime history.

Lunch
There are plenty of lunch places here as you're back on the continuation of the **Riva degli Schiavoni** (▷ 71)—head for the good value places on Via Garibaldi or cut though to **Da Remigio** (▷ 147) for a quintessentially Venetian eating experience at this traditional restaurant.

Afternoon
Now is the time to take in the glowing pictures in the **Scuola di San Giorgio degli Schiavoni** (▷ 60–61), before heading west to contrast this with the artistic treasures in **San Zaccaria** (▷ 44–45).

Mid-afternoon
You could relax after this by taking the *vaporetto* to **Giardini**, an area of cool trees, benches and green open spaces, part of which is home to the permanent buildings used during Venice's annual Biennale art shows, showcasing art and architecture in alternate years.

Evening
Don't miss a pre-dinner drink on the waterfront (left), with views across St. Mark's Basin to the island of **San Giorgio Maggiore** (▷ 40–41).

Dinner
Castello has some of the best restaurants in Venice; try the old-established and renowned **Corte Sconta** (▷ 147; right), the superb **Osteria alle Testiere** (▷ 149) or the **Osteria Oliva Nera** (▷ 150), where you'll find the best of contemporary Venetian cooking.

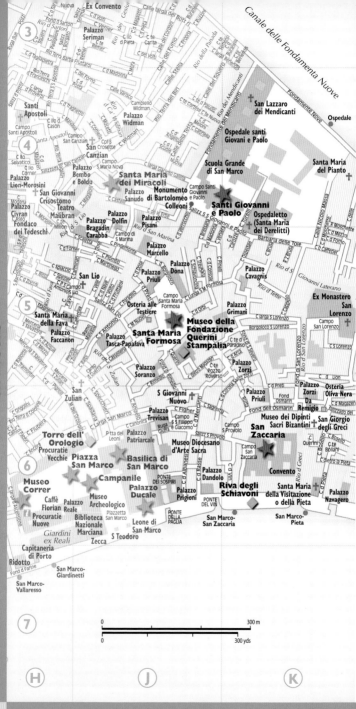

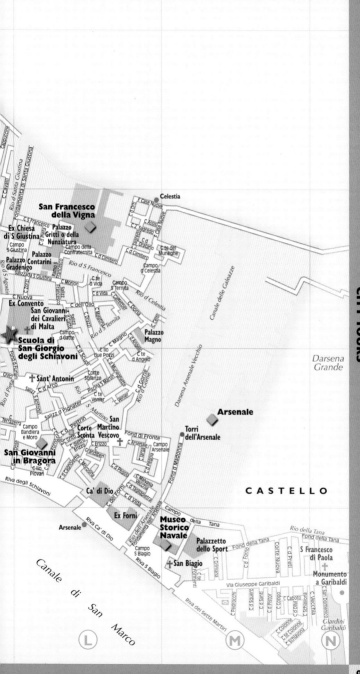

San Francesco
della Vigna

Ex Chiesa
di S Giustina

Palazzo
Gritti o della
Nunziatura

Campo
S Giustina

Palazzo
Contarini
Gradenigo

Ex Convento

San Giovanni
dei Cavalieri
di Malta

Scuola di
San Giorgio
degli Schiavoni

Celestia

C Casse Nuove

Campo della
Confraternita

C te del
Muneghe

Campo
d Celestia

Palazzo
Magno

Canale delle Galeazze

Darsena
Grande

Sant' Antonin

San
Martino
Vescovo

Corte
Sconta

Arsenale

Torri
dell'Arsenale

San Giovanni
in Bragora

Darsena Arsenale Vecchio

Riva degli Schiavoni

CASTELLO

Ca' di Dio

Ex Forni

Arsenale

Riva Ca' di Dio

Museo
Storico
Navale

Campo
della
Tana

Rio della Tana

Fond della Tana

S Francesco
di Paola

Palazzetto
dello Sport

Campo
S Biagio

Riva S Biagio

San Biagio

Via Giuseppe Garibaldi

Monumento
a Garibaldi

Canale   di   San   Marco

Riva del Sette Martiri

Giardini
Garibaldi

L

M

N

SIGHTS AND EXPERIENCES

San Zaccaria (▷ 44)

San Zaccaria dates from the ninth century, though what you see now, essentially two adjacent churches, is a blend of both Gothic and Renaissance styles. Inside, look out for Giovanni Bellini's *Madonna and Child with Saints* (1505), and don't miss the chance to inspect Venice's only crypt.

Santa Maria Formosa (▷ 46)

This interesting church and its *campo* is archetypical Venice—diverse architecture, a lively square that's the hub of the neighborhood, and one of Venice's most beguiling museums. The Byzantine 11th-century church was altered in 1492 by Mauro Codussi in the new Renaissance style.

Santi Giovanni e Paolo (▷ 54)

This huge Gothic preaching church is typical of those built by the mendicant religious orders, with a cavernous interior designed to accommodate huge crowds. It's the burial place of more than 20 doges, and contains some of the city's best sculpture. The highlights are on the west wall.

Scuola di San Giorgio degli Schiavoni (▷ 60)

Tucked away on a side canal, this charitable *scuola* is home to some of the most charming paintings in the city, a cycle by Carpaccio, painted in the first decade of the 16th century. You'll recognize St. George slaying the dragon, while the terrified princess looks on.

CITY TOURS

Sunrise over the Riva degli Schiavoni

San Polo and Santa Croce

Enclosed by a loop of the upper stretches of the Canal Grande, the west-bank *sestieri* of San Polo and Santa Croce are densely populated, workaday districts, where there's a tangible sense of Venice as a living city. The Rialto, with its superb fish and fruit and vegetable markets, is the focus, with the big sights mainly lying south of here, among them fine churches and museums, while the whole area has good shopping and great bars and restaurants.

Morning

Start your day—and miss the worst of the crowds—by taking the *vaporetto* along the **Canal Grande** (▷ 20–21; right), alighting at San Tomà, the nearest stop to the great church of **Santa Maria Gloriosa dei Frari** (▷ 48–49), where you'll find plenty to fill in 40 minutes or so.

Mid-morning

You'll find good choices for a mid-morning stop on the Campo dei Frari—try **Bottega del Caffè Dersut** (▷ 146), where there are delicious smoothies, as well as excellent coffee, on offer. Then stroll round the side of the Frari to take in the mind-blowing architecture, incredible interior decoration and superb paintings by Tintoretto in the **Scuola Grande di San Rocco** (▷ 58–59).

Lunch

You could follow the main route up towards the Rialto and sit beside the Canal Grande for lunch at **Bancogiro** (▷ 146; left), where there's a choice of *cichetti* (Venetian-style tapas) as well as a full menu. Alternatively, choose somewhere in Campo San Polo, Venice's second largest square.

Afternoon

After lunch, you'll want to browse the stalls around the **Rialto bridge** (▷ 38–39), good trawling ground for gifts and souvenirs. Later, take the *vaporetto* towards Piazzale Roma from Rialto Mercato, and get off at San Stae, from where you can visit two important museums, **Ca' Pesaro** (▷ 66–67), a magnificent *palazzo* housing the city's modern art collection, or **Palazzo Mocenigo** (▷ 70–71; left), home to a fascinating collection of costumes displayed in a great palace.

Mid-afternoon

From Palazzo Mocenigo it's a short stroll to **San Giacomo dell'Orio** (▷ 71–72; right), a fascinating church on a *campo* that's a good place to sit and relax with a drink. Explore the little streets around here, where you'll find tiny specialist shops and hidden corners.

Evening

If you haven't already taken it in, you can cut through from here to Campo San Polo to take in the church of **San Polo** (▷ 73–74) before joining the locals who congregate here for the early evening *passeggiata*.

Dinner

There's a great choice of restaurants to suit all tastes and pockets in the area—go upmarket and enjoy stunning modern cuisine at the **Antiche Carampane** (▷ 146), head for **Alla Madonna** (▷ 144), one of Venice's most famous and traditional fish restaurants, or enjoy an excellent pizza at **Il Refolo** (▷ 150), back on Campo San Giacomo dell'Orio.

0   300 m

0   300 yds

STAZIONE
VENEZIA
SANTA LUCIA

SANTA
CROCE

2
3
4
5
6

D   **E**

Canal Grande

Giardini
Savorgnan

Giardino
Papadopoli

Piazzale
Roma

Campazzo
Tre Ponti

Palazzo
Nani

Tempio
Israelitico

Palazzo
Savorgnan

Palazzo
Venier   Guglie

Rio Terra S Leonardo

Campo
S Leonardo

Ex Chiesa
di San Leonardo

Palazzo
Labia

San Geremia
e Lucia

Palazzo
Emo

Palazzo
Gritti
Contarini

Palazzo
Correr
Contarini

Palazzo
Giovanelli

Palazzo
Marcello
Toderini

Palazzo
Gidoni-
Bembo

Chiesa degli
Scalzi

Palazzo
Calbo-Crotta

Palazzo
Flangini

Riva de
Biasio

Palazzo
Corner

Palazzo
Gritti

Palazzo
Dona-
Balbi

San Giovanni
Decollato

Il Réfolo

San Giacomo
dell' Orio

Ferrovia

Ponte
degli Scalzi

Case
Contarini

Palazzo
Foscari

S Simeon
Piccolo

Palazzo
Adoldo

Palazzo
Gradenigo

S Simeon
Grande

Palazzo
Soranzo
Cappello

Palazzo
Mariani

Palazzo
Emo-Diedo

Ponte della
Costituzione
(Calatrava)

Palazzo
Papadopoli

Palazzo
Zane-Collalto

Palazzo
Giustinian

Palazzo
Molin

Scuola Grande di
San Giovanni
Evangelista

San Giovanni
Evangelista

Palazzo
Zen

Palazzo
Condulmer

San Nicolo
da Tolentino

Archivio
di Stato

San
Rocco

Santa Maria
Gloriosa dei Frari

Palazzo
Marcello

Scuola
Grande
di San
Rocco

Bottega del
Caffè Dersut

Museo Casa Carlo
Goldoni

Palazzo
Gabrieli Dolfin

San
Pantaleone

Palazzo
Dolfin

Palazzo
Signolo
Loredan

Palazzo Marcello
dei Leoni

Palazzo
Civran Grimani

San
Toma

Palazzo
Balbi

Palazzo
Contarini
delle Figure

Palazzo
Foscarini

Palazzo
Da Lezze

Ca' Foscari

Palazzo
Giustinian

Palazzo
Morolin

Campo Santa
Margherita

Scuola
del Varotari

Palazzo
Nani

Palazzo
Grassi

San
Samuele

Institiuto Superiore
d'Arte Applicata

Scuola Grande
dei Carmini

Ca' Rezzonico

Ca'
Rezzonico

Palazzo
Malipiero

Palazzo
Cicogna

Santa Maria
dei Carmini

San Barnaba

Palazzo
Contarini-
Michiel

Ca' del
Duca

Collegio
Armeno

Palazzo
Moro

Palazzo
Loredan

Palazzo Falier

102

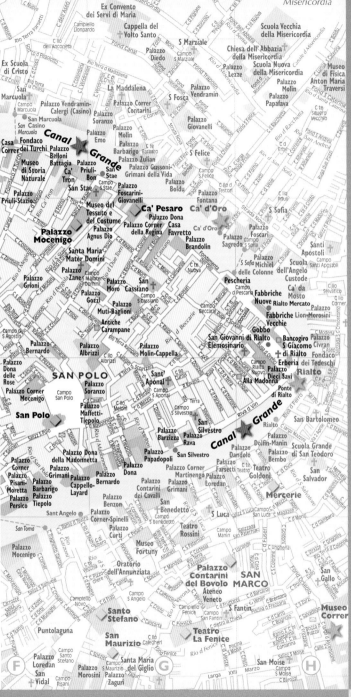

Sacca della Misericordia

Ex Convento dei Servi di Maria
Cappella del Volto Santo
S Marziale
Scuola Vecchia della Misericordia
Chiesa della Abbazia della Misericordia
Scuola Nuova della Misericordia
Museo di Fisica Anton Maria Traversi
Ex Scuola di Cristo
Palazzo Diedo
Fond Canal
Campo S Marziale
Palazzo Lezze
Palazzo Molin
Palazzo Papafava
La Maddalena
Palazzo Correr Contarini
S Fosca
Palazzo Vendramin
San Marcuola
Palazzo Vendramin-Calergi (Casino)
Palazzo Soranzo
Palazzo Giovanelli
Casa Correr
Fondaco dei Turchi
San Marcuola
San Casino Marcuola
Palazzo Emo
Palazzo Molin
Museo di Storia Naturale
Palazzo Belloni Battagia
Ca' Tron
Palazzo Priuli-Bon
San Stae
Palazzo Barbarigo
S Felice
Canal Grande
Palazzo Priuli-Stazio
San Stae
Palazzo Zulian
Palazzo Gussoni-Grimani della Vida
Palazzo Boldu
Palazzo Testori
Palazzo Foscarini-Giovanelli
Museo del Tessuto e del Costume
Ca' Pesaro
Palazzo Dona
Ca' d'Oro
Palazzo Mocenigo
Palazzo Agnus Dio
Palazzo Corner della Regina
Casa Favretto
Ca' d'Oro
Palazzo Foscari Sagredo
Santi Apostoli
Santa Maria Mater Domini
Palazzo Brandolin
Scuola Santi Apostoli
Palazzo Grioni
Palazzo Zane
S Sofia Michiel delle Colonne
Palazzo Sofia
Ca' da Mosto
Palazzo Moro
San Cassiano
Pescheria
Fabbriche Nuove
Rialto Mercato
Palazzo Gozzi
Campo San Cassiano
Fabbriche Vecchie
Lion-Morosini
Muti-Baglioni
Gobbo
Antiche Carampane
San Giovanni di Rialto Elemosinario
Bancogiro
Palazzo Civran
Palazzo Bernardo
Palazzo Albrizzi
Palazzo Molin-Cappella
S Giacomo di Rialto
Fondaco
Erberia dei Tedeschi
Palazzo Dona delle Rose
SAN POLO
Palazzo Soranzo
Sant' Aponal
Dieci Savi
Rialto
Palazzo Corner Mocenigo
Campo San Polo
Palazzo Maffetti-Tiepolo
Alla Madonna
Ponte di Rialto
San Polo
Palazzo Dona della Madonnetta
San Silvestro
Canal Grande
San Bartolomeo
Palazzo Corner
Palazzo Grimani
Palazzo Barzizza
Palazzo Rava
Rialto
Palazzo Dolfin-Manin
Scuola Grande di San Teodoro
Palazzo Pisani-Moretta
Palazzo Barbarigo
Palazzo Cappello-Layard
Palazzo Bernardo
Palazzo Papadopoli
San Silvestro
Palazzo Dandolo
Palazzo Bembo
Palazzo Persico
Palazzo Tiepolo
Palazzo Benzon
Palazzo Corner Martinengo
Palazzo Farsetti
Teatro Goldoni
San Salvador
Sant Angelo
Palazzo Contarini dei Cavalli
San Benedetto
Palazzo Loredan
Palazzo Grimani
Mercerie
San Toma
Palazzo Corner-Spinelli
S Luca
Palazzo Mocenigo
Palazzo Curti
Teatro Rossini
Campo Manin
SAN MARCO
San Gallo
Museo Fortuny
Oratorio dell'Annunziata
Palazzo Contarini del Bovolo
San Salvatore
Museo Correr
Ateneo Veneto
Santo Stefano
Puntolaguna
San Maurizio
Santa Maria del Giglio
Teatro La Fenice
S Fantin
San Moise
Palazzo Loredan
San Vidal
Palazzo Morosini
Palazzo Zaguri
Larga XXII Marzo
Campo S Moise

F   G   H

San Polo and Santa Croce
Quick Reference Guide

CITY TOURS

Canal Grande (▷ 20)

If you do nothing else in Venice, take a *vaporetto* trip down this iconic waterway, which winds for 4km (2.5 miles) from Piazzale Roma to the glories of San Marco, with a spectacular pageant of some of the world's most beautiful buildings rising from the water on either side. Spanned by four bridges, the canal is lined with *palazzi* and churches whose architecture spans many styles.

Santa Maria Gloriosa dei Frari (▷ 48)

This impressive church, dating from the 13th century, was built for the Franciscans. Completed around 1395, the lofty interior contains masterpieces by some of Venice's greatest artists. Don't miss Titian's *Assumption of the Virgin* over the high altar, his *Madonna di Ca' Pesaro* in the left aisle, or Giovanni Bellini's triptych of the *Madonna and Child* in the sacristy.

Scuola Grande di San Rocco (▷ 58)

This headquarters of a charitable institution, or *scuola,* built between 1515 and 1549, was designed by Bartolomeow Bon. The interior is the perfect backdrop for the mind-blowing pictures by Tintoretto. His 54 paintings, on two floors, are one of the world's most impressive picture cycles by a single artist. Other works are by Titian, Giorgione, Bellini and Tiepolo.

CITY TOURS

Dorsoduro

Lying to the southwest of the Canal Grande, Dorsoduro's name means "hard back," referring to the firm land on which it stands. Its southern boundary is the Giudecca canal, edged by the long stretch of the sunny Zattere, its hub, lovely Campo Santa Margherita. It's a compelling *sestiere*, with three important galleries, superb churches, *palazzi* and *campi*, while the University lends a buzz and ensures good shopping, lively bars and a choice of restaurants.

Morning
You could start your day early with an overview of Venetian painting by taking in the **Gallerie dell'Accademia** (▷ 24–25). Be sure to climb the steps of the **Ponte dell'Accademia** (▷ 71; right) for one of the finest of all Venetian views, down the Canal Grande towards Santa Maria della Salute.

Mid-morning
Wend your way eastwards through picturesque *calli* and *campi* to the **Collezione Peggy Guggenheim** (▷ 22–23) where you could have a drink at the excellent café before taking in the *palazzo* and the art collections. From here, it's a short walk to the **Punta della Dogana** (▷ 36–37; left) and the church of **Santa Maria della Salute** (▷ 52–53).

Lunch
From Santa Maria della Salute it's a pleasant stroll along the Zattere, where there are plenty of lunch choices. Turn off at Rio San Trovaso for the **Cantina del Vino Già Schiavi** with its fine range of *cichetti* (a Venetian version of tapas), or sit and eat a pizza or simple lunch at one of the terrace restaurants on the Zattere itself.

Afternoon

Head back to **Ca' Rezzonico** (▷ 18–19) for a taste of hedonistic 18th-century interior design, before an afternoon trawling the charming backstreets of Dorsoduro. You could head to **San Sebastiano** (▷ 42–43; left), with its great Veronese paintings, or take in the lower-key charms of the contrasting churches of **San Nicolò dei Mendicoli** (▷ 73) or the **Angelo Raffaele** (▷ 66).

Mid-afternoon

Aim to finish your stroll by heading past the **Squero di San Trovaso** (▷ 75) to the Zattere, where you can buy one of the city's best ice creams at **Nico** (▷ 149), to enjoy on a bench looking across to the Giudecca.

Evening

Hit the tempting shops, to buy or browse, before heading to **Campo Santa Margherita** (▷ 67; left) where you can sit with a drink outside **Orange** (▷ 137), or one of the other bars, and soak up the atmosphere of this most appealing *campo*.

Dinner

Dorsoduro has restaurants for every taste and pocket, but among the nicest is **Antica Locanda Montin** (▷ 145), a long-established restaurant with a beautiful garden, that specializes in traditional Venetian cuisine. Then it's time for a nightcap—the **Zattere** is lovely at night with the lights of the Giudecca twinkling across the water.

Santa Chiara

Piazzale Roma

Ponte della Costituzione (Calatrava)

Emo-Diedo

Soranzo Cappello

Rio di Cristo

Palazzo Papadopoli

Campo di Cao Nuovo

Rio di Lana

Rio de S. Zuane

Scuola Grande di San Giovanni Evangelista

Canale

Ex Chiesa di Sant'Andrea

Campo s Andrea

Autorimessa

STAZIONE AUTOBUS

Piazzale Roma

Giardino Papadopoli

Palazzo Condulmer

San Giovanni Evangelista

SANTA CROCE

Piazzale Roma

Campazzo Tre Ponti

Campo s Andrea

San Nicolo da Tolentino

Palazzo Marcello

Santa Maria Gloriosa dei Frari

San Rocco

Scuola Grande di San Rocco

Campo S Rocco

Ex Chiesa di Santa Maria Maggiore

Palazzo Gabrielli Dolfin

San Pantaleone

Campo S Pantalon

Palazzo Signolo Loredan

Palazzo Foscarini

Santa Margherita

Campo Santa Margherita

Ca' Foscari

Palazzo Giustinian

Palazzo Nani

S Teresa

Palazzo Ariani

Scuola dei Varotari

Orange

Scuola Grande dei Carmini

Ca' Rezzonico

Palazzo Bernardo

Santa Maria dei Carmini

Collegio Armeno

PONTE dei PUGNI

San Barnaba

Campo San Barnaba

Palazzo Contarini-Michiel

San Nicolò dei Mendicoli

Angelo Raffaele

Campo Angelo Raffaele

Campo dietro al Cimitero

Rio di Malpaga

Rio di S

San Sebastiano

DORSODURO

Ospedale G B Giustinian

Ognissanti

Palazzo Brandolin

TERMINAL CROCIERE SAN BASILIO

Campo S Basegio

Campo Ognissanti

Montin

San Trovaso

Palazzo Nani

Palazzo Molin

San Basilio

STAZIONE MARITTIMA

Campo S Trovaso

Squero di San Trovaso

Fond Zattere al Ponte Lungo

S Maria d Visitazione

Nico

Zattere

Canale della Giudecca

Campo s Biagio

Ex Mulino Stucky

Fond S Biagio

Isola della Giudecca

Canale dei Lavraneri

Campo d Lavraneri

Rio delle Convertite

S Eufemia

Palanca

Ex Convento delle Convertite (Penitenziario Femminile)

Campo S Cosmo

Ex Chiesa Santi Cosma e Damiano

Campo delle Rotonda

4

5

6

7

8

9

C

D

E

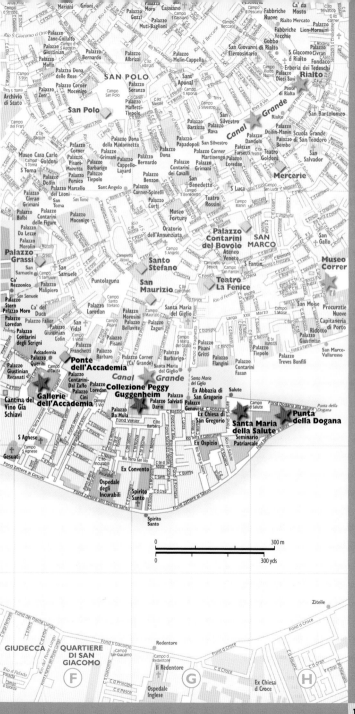

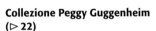

CITY TOURS

Ca' Rezzonico (▷ 18)
Come to this magnificently opulent *palazzo* for a glimpse of the lifestyle of the 18th-century Venetian nobility.

Collezione Peggy Guggenheim (▷ 22)
Get an overview of all the main artistic movements of the second half of the 20th century.

Gallerie dell'Accademia (▷ 24)
An intimate gallery that takes you through the development of Venetian painting and showcases the work of the greatest painters.

Punta della Dogana (▷ 36)
This stunningly restored building, the best of 21st-century design, is home to changing exhibitions of cutting-edge contemporary art.

San Sebastiano (▷ 42)
A church that's a shrine to the great painter Veronese, who decorated virtually the entire interior.

Santa Maria della Salute (▷ 52)
This landmark church was built in the 18th century following an outbreak of the plague in Venice.

Scuola Grande dei Carmini (▷ 56)
See some of Tiepolo's best work in this intimate setting, designed by Baldassare Longhena.

Farther Afield

Venice's lagoon, 50km (31 miles) long, is scattered with numerous other islands, and most visitors spend time exploring at least some of them. These two itineraries explore the best, and both will need forward planning as *vaporetti* run less frequently to outlying areas.

DAY 1
Morning

Start your day with a visit to **Murano** (▷ 28–29; right), taking the No. 3 from Piazzale Roma or Ferrovia, or a boat from the Fondamente Nove. If you take this route, you could hop off for a short visit to the fascinating cemetery island of **San Michele** (▷ 69). On Murano, be sure to visit one of the glass factories, where you can watch glass-blowers at work, or visit the **Museo del Vetro** (▷ 29) to learn more. Then take the No. 12 *vaporetto* from the Faro stop for the 40-minute journey to **Burano** (▷ 76).

Lunch

Burano has a good choice for lunch; try **Da Romano** (tel 041 735 217) or **Al Gatto Nero** (tel 041 730 120), both renowned for fish. After lunch, take a stroll round Burano, perhaps stopping off at the **Museo del Merletto** (▷ 76).

Afternoon

Back at the *vaporetto* stop, catch the No. 9 service for the short hop to **Torcello** (▷ 62–63), where you can visit the **Basilica di Santa Maria Assunta** (▷ 63; left) and church of **Santa Fosca** (▷ 63). You'll have to take the 9 line back to Burano to return to Venice.

Evening

The nicest route back to the city in summer is the No. 14 via Treporti and Punta Sabbioni, which gives you a chance to see more of the lagoon en route to the Lido. Change *vaporetti* here to return to Venice, either before or after dinner.

DAY 2
Morning
Catch *vaporetto* No. 2 to **San Giorgio Maggiore** (▷ 40–41; left) to visit Palladio's superb church, starting by taking the lift up the campanile for views over Venice and the lagoon islands. From June to mid-September, the No. 2 runs from San Giorgio to the **Lido** (▷ 76), where you're heading next. During other months, you'll have to return to San Zaccaria and change to the No. 1.

Lunch
Once on the Lido, there's plenty of choices for lunch on and just off the Gran Viale, which runs across the island from the lagoon to the open Adriatic. The Lido's **beaches** are a big draw; some have private facilities and are ticket only, others are free, so you could have a swim and a couple of hours on the beach if the weather's good.

Afternoon
Alternatively, take the 5.1 to the Fondamente Nove, where you connect with the No. 13 to the island of **Sant'Erasmo** (▷ 76; right). Here, you can walk for miles through vegetable fields and beside the lagoon. Disembark either at Capannone—if you want a good long walk—or Chiesa, and simply follow your nose along the island to eventually catch the boat back to Venice from the Punta Vela stop.

Favaro Veneto

Tessera

CASONA

la Cerva

VIA MARTIRI DELLA LIBERTÀ

VIA ORLANDA

Aeroporto
Marco Polo

Mestre

BISSUOLA

VIA PIAVE

VIA BISSUOLA

Calzavara

Canale Osellino

Punta
Lunga

VILLAGGIO
S MARCO

VIA A.VESPUCCI

Campalto

Stazione
Venezia Mestre

VIA F.LLI BANDIERA

VIA D. LIBERTÀ

Marghera

Porto di
Compalto

Isola di
Tessera

S Giuliano

Isola di
Campalto

L a g u n a

PONTE DELLA LIBERTÀ

Sacca
Serenella

I S Secondo

**Isola di
San Michele**

Porto
Marghera

Nuova Isola
del Tronchetto

Stazione
Venezia
Santa Lucia

Moranzani

I d Tresse

VENEZIA

**San Giorgio
Maggiore**

Navíglio Brenta

Canale della Giudecca

Canale Bondante
di Sotto

I S Giórgio
in Alga

Isola della
Giudecca

Isola di
San Giorgio
Maggiore

Fusina

I La Grázia

V e n e t a

I S Ángelo

I S Clemente

Sacca
Séssola

I S Spirito

Lago
dei
Téneri

L a g u n a

Isola Forte
di Sopra

Isola
Povéglia

Isola Forte
di Mezzo

MALAMOCCO

Isola Forte
di Sotto

L di Rívola

0   4 km

ALBERONI

0   2 miles

Porto di
Malamocco

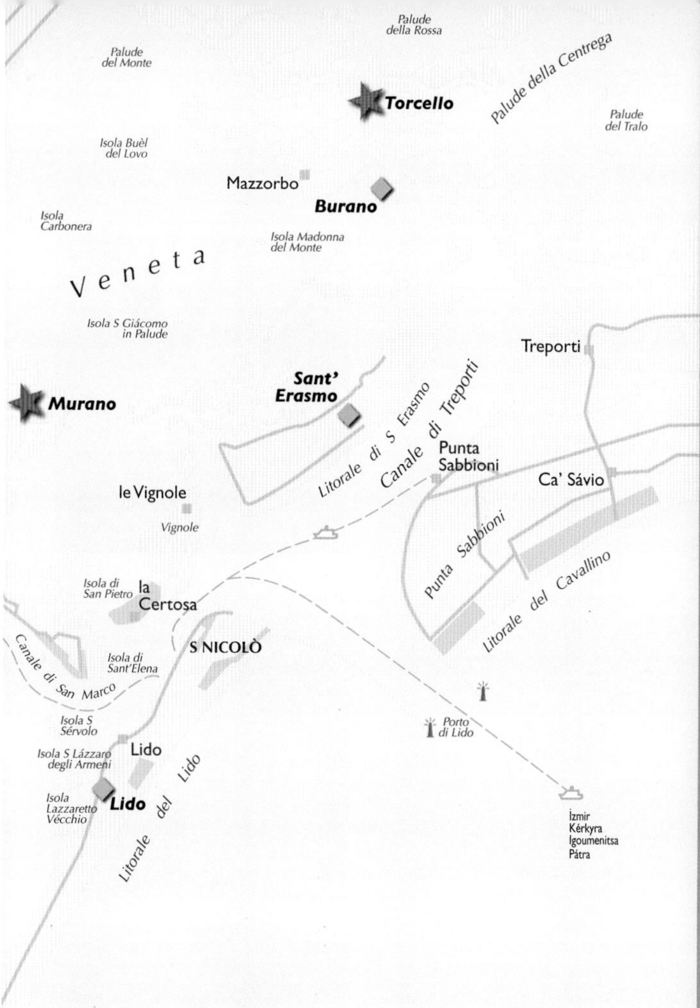

Palude
del Monte

Palude della Centrega

Palude
del Tralo

Torcello

Isola Buèl
del Lovo

Mazzorbo

Burano

Isola
Carbonera

Isola Madonna
del Monte

V e n e t a

Isola S Giácomo
in Palude

Treporti

Sant'
Erasmo

Litorale di S Erasmo

Canale di Treporti

Murano

Punta
Sabbioni

Ca' Sávio

le Vignole

Vignole

Punta Sabbioni

Litorale del Cavallino

Isola di
San Pietro

la
Certosa

Canale di San Marco

Isola di
Sant'Elena

S NICOLÒ

Isola S
Sérvolo

Porto
di Lido

Isola S Lázzaro
degli Armeni

Lido

Isola
Lazzaretto
Vécchio

Lido

Litorale del Lido

İzmir
Kérkyra
Igoumenitsa
Pátra

CITY TOURS

Farther Afield Quick Reference Guide

CITY TOURS

Murano (▷ 28)

Ten minutes by *vaporetto* from Venice, the island of Murano, complete with its own canals, churches and *palazzi*, has been the center of Venetian glass manufacture since the Middle Ages. The Museo del Vetro tells the story and you can watch glass-blowing in the workshops. The beautiful 12th-century church of Santa Maria e Donato is another highlight.

San Giorgio Maggiore (▷ 40)

Across the Bacino di San Marco from the Palazzo Ducale, the little island of San Giorgio Maggiore (opposite) is dominated by the great Palladian church of the same name and its adjoining monastic buildings. Built between 1565 and 1610, the classical design shines with white marble and stucco, while the view from the campanile is one of Venice's finest.

Torcello (▷ 62)

More than an hour's journey from the city, in the wastes of the northern lagoon, once heavily populated Torcello is home to an exquisite ninth-century Basilica, the oldest complete building in Venice, famous for its superb Byzantine mosaics. The island is also home to the church of 11th-century Santa Fosca and a small museum.

MORE TO SEE	64

Burano	The Lido
Isola di San Michele	Sant'Erasmo

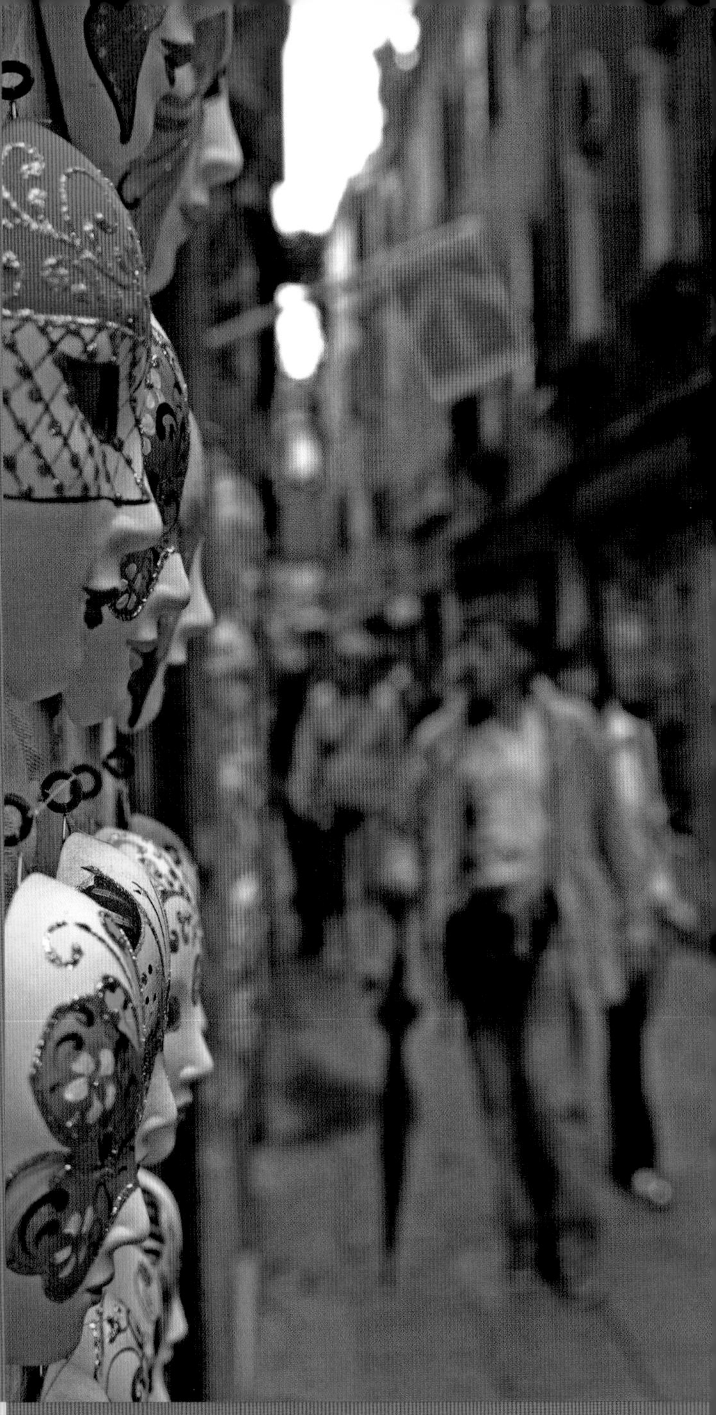

Shop

Whether you're looking for the best local products, a department store or a quirky boutique, you'll find them all in Venice. In this section shops are listed alphabetically.

SHOP

Introduction

Venice was one of the world's greatest trading hubs for 500 years before its decline in the 17th and 18th centuries. Sumptuous goods from all corners of the globe filled its markets, shops and warehouses. Today, its trade is less exotic but often still tempting.

On Offer
Venice is a provincial city and its shops reflect this, though you'll find many designer names and some great Italian fashion, accessories and shoes. Transportation costs and high rents also mean prices are often higher than elsewhere.

Traditional Gifts
Venice's extraordinary history has bequeathed the city several unique shopping possibilities. The artisan traditions of Murano and Burano, for example, make glass and lace from these two lagoon islands good buys—though you must be on your guard against inferior, foreign-produced products. Glass trinkets can also provide some of Venice's most kitsch souvenirs.

Beautiful Masks
With the revival of the Venice carnival in 1979, the last few years has seen shops selling and producing the traditional masks *(maschere)* worn by celebrants proliferating. Some masks are mass-produced—but often still beautiful—while others are painstakingly created by hand

BURANO LACE

Although lace was made by women of all classes during the Middle Ages, it was the development of an intricate stitch known as Burano point that made the eponymous island (▷ 76) famous for its lace. Mass production in the 19th century devastated the industry, and today only a handful of women make lace by hand. Much of what you see for sale in Burano and the rest of Venice is foreign- or machine-made. For the real thing you will have to search long and hard and be prepared to pay.

Clockwise from top: Masks hanging outside a shop; lace parasols in Burano; the Rialto fish market; a shop window display of Murano glass; hand-printed paper in

in workshops, such as Tragicomica (▷ 129) around the city. Locally produced masks fetch high prices, but they do make the most wonderful souvenirs.

Stationery Delights

Marbled paper, another traditional Venetian craft, has also enjoyed a revival since the 1970s and shops across the city sell a range of paper products. The craft is almost 1,000 years old, and spread from Japan to Persia and the Arab world during the Middle Ages. It reached Europe in about the 15th century. Mass-produced papers are perfectly good, but the best buys are authentic, made using old hand- and woodblock-printing techniques.

Delicate Materials

Shops selling a host of fine silks, damasks and other fabrics reflect the city's trading days. And as you'd expect in a city with such an illustrious artistic past, there are many antiques shops filled with beautiful paintings, prints and objets d'art (▷ panel, 125).

And to Eat

Food souvenirs include pasta in every shape and form, rice and polenta, olive oil, dried *porcini* (mushrooms), vinegars, spices and traditional Burano biscuits.

SHOP

MURANO GLASS

Glass-making began in Venice in Roman times, but took off in the 13th century, when foundries were moved to Murano (▷ 28–29) to lessen the risk of fire. Today, the island is a key production area; though shops sell Murano glass everywhere in Venice, the best choice, and keenest prices, are on the island. With its ornate forms and many tints, Murano glass is an acquired taste but the huge variety of styles includes both contemporary and traditional designs. At its best, glass is one of the city's most distinctive buys.

---

a range of designs; the view from the Rialto bridge towards Campo San Bartolomeo

121

Directory

SHOP

Shopping A–Z

ALIANI GASTRONOMIA
Perhaps Venice's most famous delicatessen, this shop has a superlative selection of cheeses, and a variety of hams, salamis, fresh pasta and other ready-made delicacies—all perfect for a picnic.
🟦 G5 ✉ Ruga Vecchia San Giovanni, San Polo 654 ☎ 041 522 4913 🚢 Rialto or San Silvestro N, 1, 2

ALL'OMBRA DEL VESUVIO
The menswear here may be from Naples, but it's perfectly in tune with the Venetian taste for elegance and class. The main draws are exquisite and heavy silk ties by Marinella, and cashmere sweaters and other knitwear in a rainbow of colors by Capua.
🟦 H6 ✉ Calle Fuseri, San Marco 4272 ☎ 041 523 5217 🚢 San Marco—Vallaresso 1, 2

ANTICLEA ANTIQUARIATO
This beautiful little shop is a wonderful collection of antique Venetian beads and jewelry. The owner has spent a lifetime amassing her stock, the best of which is kept in countless small drawers around the walls. Beads of your choice can be made up, while you wait, into earrings or necklaces.
🟦 K6 ✉ Campo San Provolo, Castello 4719a ☎ 041 528 6946 🚢 San Zaccaria 1, 2, 4.1, 4.2, 5.1, 5.2

BAC ART STUDIO
bacart.com
For some stunning photos of Venice to take home and prove to people that it really does look dreamlike, Bac Art Studio has an impressive range. There are also framed prints of original art, as well as ceramics, porcelain, glass, stationery and calendars.
🟦 F7 ✉ San Vio, Dorsoduro 862 ☎ 041 241 2898 🚢 Accademia N, 1, 2

BALLARIN
This excellent *pasticceria* has a superb range of cakes and pastries, to sample with a cup of coffee or take out. It also makes delicious chocolates and sweets—look out for the chocolate-coated orange peel, candied fruit and fresh cream chocolate truffles.

Confectionery in a shop window on Campo San Luca

🚩 H4 ✉ Salizzada San Giovanni Crisostomo, Cannaregio 5794 ☎ 041 528 5273 🚊 Rialto N, 1, 2

BARBIERI ARABESQUE

This elegant shop sells nothing but scarves, stoles and pashminas in silk, wool, cashmere and a great range of hues and styles; all tracked down by the English-speaking owner, who has excellent contacts in the silk-weaving towns around Lake Garda. Scarves for dressing up, keeping you warm and adding individuality and luxury to any outfit.

🚩 K6 ✉ Ponte dei Greci, Castello 3403 ☎ 041 522 8177 🚊 San Zaccaria 1, 2, 4.1, 4.2, 5.1, 5.2

CAMPO MARZIO

campomarzio.it

Campo Marzio stores specialize in brilliantly colored leather goods, with a particular emphasis on writing and desk accessories. Styles range from classic to funky, and you'll find carrying cases for writing papers, documents and even headphones, while the braided leather key rings make great gifts. They also make beautiful pens.

🚩 G6 ✉ Calle della Mandola, San Marco 3546/a ☎ 041 522 0508 🚊 Sant'Angelo 2

CASA DEL PARMIGIANO

aliani-casadelparmigiano.it

A stone's-throw from the Rialto markets, this delightful little family-run shop sells superb cheese in excellent condition, a huge range of *salumeria* (delicatessen) from all over Italy and light-as-a-feather home-made fresh pasta. Locals consider this one of the best shops for gastronomic specialties in Venice, so be prepared to stand in line.

🚩 H5 ✉ Erberia, San Polo 214–15 ☎ 041 520 6525 🚊 Rialto N, 1, 2

CLAUDIA CANESTRELLI

This tiny shop sells old prints, ornaments and lamps, but its chief draw are the beautiful 18th-century-style drop earrings made by the owner. Decorated with pearls, tiny rubies and emeralds, they are surprisingly good value.

🚩 G7 ✉ Campiello Barbaro, Dorsoduro 364A ☎ 041 522 7072 🚊 Accademia 1, 2 or Salute 1

COLORCASA

This shop is crammed with some of the most sumptuous decorating fabrics you can imagine—silks, brocades and figured velvets are for sale by the length or made up into cushions, drapes and bags. Silk key tassels and curtain swags are equally tempting, and ColorCasa stocks wonderfully warm *trapunti* (quilted bed-covers) in vivid fabrics.

🚩 F5 ✉ Campo San Polo, San Polo 1989–91 ☎ 041 523 6071 🚊 San Tomà N, 1, 2

MARIANO FORTUNY

Fortuny was born in Catalonia, Spain in 1871, the son of a painter and fabric collector. He moved to Venice when he was 18, soon gaining renown in fields ranging from physics and chemistry to architecture and theater design. Today, he is best remembered for his fabrics, and in particular for the pleated dresses he created that were so fine they could be rolled up and threaded through a wedding ring.

EBRÛ

albertovalese-ebru.it

The owner of this shop, Alberto Valese, was at the cutting edge of the 1970s revival in Venetian marbled paper. His shop takes its name from the traditional Turkish marbling technique used to create many of his products.

➕ F6 ✉ Campo Santo Stefano, San Marco 3471 ☎ 041 523 8830 🚤 Giglio 1

EMILIO CECCATO

emilioceccato.com

If there is one souvenir, over and above glass, that greets you at every turn in Venice, it is the fake and mass-produced gondolier's straw hat. This unique little shop sells the genuine article, together with gondoliers' garb—hats, tunics and trousers—to both gondoliers and curious foreigners.

➕ H5 ✉ Sottoportego di Rialto, San Polo 1617 ☎ 041 522 2700 🚤 Rialto N, 1, 2

F.G.B.

fgb-muranoglass.com

This long-established store, housed in a charming *casinetto* in the center of the *campo*, sells all the traditional Venetian souvenirs at some of the best prices in town. There are glass pieces in clear and milk colors, beads and earrings, paper products and much more besides, and there's plenty for children that won't break the bank.

➕ G7 ✉ Campo Santa Maria del Giglio, San Marco 2514 ☎ 041 523 6556 🚤 Giglio 1

FONDACO DEI TEDESCHI

tfondaco.com

Built by medieval German merchants as their Venice head-quarters, the iconic Fondaco dei

ANTIQUES

Bric-a-brac and antiques bargains are rare in a city that is acutely aware of its past and the value of its objets d'art. Still, Venice provides an almost unlimited choice of beautiful things to buy. The most famous shops in San Marco are Pietro Scarpa's two outlets at Campo San Moisè, San Marco 1464 (➕ H6) and Calle Larga (Viale) XXII Marzo, San Marco 2089 (➕ H6).

Tedeschi overlooks the Grand Canal next to the Rialto Bridge. It was used for many years as the post office and has now been stunningly and beautifully restored as a high-end shopping center, featuring every conceivable luxury brand for men and women, as well as beauty products, food and wine. There are superb views from the top terrace and an elegant bar-restaurant.

➕ H5 ✉ Calle del Fontego dei Tedeschi, San Marco 32 ☎ 041 314 2000 🚤 Rialto 1, 2

GALLERIA LIVIO DE MARCHI

liviodemarchi.com

You will probably see examples of Livio de Marchi's work as you walk around Venice: everyday objects such as socks, umbrellas or hanging shirts lovingly and precisely carved of wood. You may not want to buy the items, but the works are unique, and great fun.

➕ F6 ✉ Calle del Dose, Corte da Ponte, San Marco 2742/a ☎ 041 528 5694 🚤 Sant'Angelo or San Samuele N, 1, 2

GIANNI BASSO

Going into Gianni Basso's *stampatore* will take you back in time. The huge old printing

Beautiful Venetian handmade paper

presses are still in action, making business cards for people all over the world. Gianni has resisted change—he doesn't have a web-site and takes orders by mail only. He also sells beautiful lithographs of Venice then and now.

🔲 J2 ⊠ Calle del Fumo, Cannaregio 5306 ☎ 041 523 4681 🚤 Fondamente Nove N, 1, 4.1, 4.2, 5.1, 5.2, 13

GILBERTO PENZO

veniceboats.com

What more appropriate gift or souvenir to take home from Venice than a gondola? This shop sells beautiful handmade wooden mod-els of the boats, as well as gondola prints, posters and simple models (perfect for children) either as kits or ready-made and painted.

🔲 F5 ⊠ Calle Il Saoneri, San Polo 2681 ☎ 041 524 6139 🚤 San Tomà N, 1, 2

GOLDONI

Well stocked and by common con-sent the best general bookshop in Venice, Goldoni has a wide range of literature on the city, along with a limited selection of English and other foreign-language titles.

🔲 H6 ⊠ Calle dei Fabbri, San Marco 4742 ☎ 041 522 2384 🚤 Vallaresso N, 1, 2

JESURUM

jesurum.it

Jesurum have been making some of the most exquisite household linens in the world since the 19th century. There are sheets, towels, tableware, pillows, cushions and throws, all of the finest linen and cotton and edged with lace or trimmed with beautiful bindings. Designs are both classic and contemporary.

🔲 G6 ⊠ Calle Veste, San Marco 2025 ☎ 041 523 8969 🚤 Giglio 1 or Sant'Angelo 2

LEGATORIA PIAZZESI

legatoriapiazzesi.it

Established in 1900, this is one of the last workshops in the city to use traditional wood-block meth-ods to hand-print its exceptionally fine papers, books and stationery.

🔲 G6 ⊠ Campiello della Feltrina, San Marco 2511 ☎ 041 522 1202 🚤 Giglio 1

DEPARTMENT STORE

The only large department store worthy of the name is the excellent Coin, which sells a wide range of fashion, toiletries, beauty products, often at excellent prices, accessories, china, linen, gifts and general goods. The staff win the prize for being among the most engaging shop assistants in Venice. It occupies a large corner block on the east side of Salizzada San Giovanni Crisostomo 5790 between the Rialto and the church of San Giovanni Crisostomo (🔲 H4).

This small but atmospheric market (⏰ Mon–Sat 8–1), just outside the north gates of the Via Garibaldi (gardens), sells fish, *salumeria* (cooked and cured meats), fruit and vegetables. If you are visiting the Museo Storico Navale or the Biennale, it is worth taking a look and enjoying a relatively tourist-free experience; if you're buying, prices are among the city's lowest.

LEGATORIA POLLIERO

This tiny, old-fashioned book-binder's studio alongside Santa Maria Gloriosa dei Frari, offers a lovely selection of leather-bound and marbled paper stationery, together with handmade gifts, prints on textiles and beautiful individual sheets of paper.

➕ F5 ✉ Campo dei Frari, San Polo 2995
☎ 041 528 5130 🚤 San Tomà N, 1, 2

LIBRERIA ACQUA ALTA

This quirky shop, close to St Mark's Square, is a one-off, with its cluttered interior dominated by a full-size gondola serving as a book display stand, and its walls stacked high with new and second-hand books, magazines and maps. The multilingual owner is a real enthusiast; the accent of the stock is on Venice, and you'll also find photos, posters and gifts. It's a must for lovers of books.

➕ J5 ✉ Calle Longa Santa Maria Formosa, Castello 5176 ☎ 041 296 0841 🚤 San Zaccaria 1, 2

LIBRERIA TOLETTA

latoletta.com

The Libreria is an excellent bookshop with a huge range of coffee-table books on Venice, guidebooks, Italian classics, art and cookery books—and they're all offered with good discount.

➕ E7 ✉ Calle Toletta, Dorsoduro 1214
☎ 041 523 2034 🚤 Ca' Rezzonico

MARCO POLO

Bruno Tagliapietra is renowned for his sumptuous and beautiful hand-blocked and figured damask velvets, made in the traditional Venetian style. Deeply and richly colored fabric is made up into cushions, runners, bedspreads, stoles and scarves—a souvenir to hand on to the next generation.

➕ M7 ✉ Via Garibaldi, Castello 1696 (if closed ask at Castello 1764 for access)
☎ 041 523 2716 🚤 Arsenale 1, 4.1, 4.2

MARINA & SUSANNA SENT

marinaesusannasent.com

For a more contemporary take on Murano glass, this shop has funky vases, plates and jewelry that won't break the bank. They sell lovely glass pebbles, too.

➕ F7 ✉ Campo San Vio, Dorsoduro 669 ☎ 041 520 8136
🚤 Accademia N, 1, 2

MURANERO

muranero.venezia.it

Niang Moulaye from Senegal became fascinated with Venetian glass-making when he came to Italy as a student. He learned the craft of bead-making and today makes beautiful, solid necklaces and bracelets in intense colors, the earthy or vibrant shades and designs inspired by Africa.

➕ L6 ✉ Salizada del Pignater, Castello 3545 ☎ 347 649 7947, 338 450 3099
🚤 Arsenale 1, 4.1, 4.2

SHOP

NICOLA TENDERINI
fontegoart.it

Nicola is a gifted watercolorist with an attractive, loose style, who sells her paintings as they are and also uses them as designs for textiles, scarves, bags, bookmarks, calendars, recipe books and cards. The shop is an excellent source for easily carried small gifts for friends back home, with a good range of prices.

✚ E7 ✉ Shop: Ramo Toletta, Dorsoduro 1183/b; studio: Campo Bella Vienna, San Polo 216 ☎ Shop: 041 523 8691; studio: 041 522 6532 🚊 Shop: Accademia/ Ca' Rezzonico 1, 2; studio: Rialto Mercato 1

O STORE
obag.it

O Store was launched in 2009 with the aim of creating watches and bags that were totally customizable and individual to each and every wearer. Mix and match from a range of 120 watch faces and 36 strap colors—the watches snap in and out of the strap. Bags can be custom made, or choose from the ever-changing selection.

✚ H4 ✉ San Giovanni Crisostomo, Cannaregio 5692 ☎ 041 522 6422 🚊 Rialto 1, 2

THE RIALTO

As a district, the Rialto is almost as old as the city itself, the earliest settlers having been attracted to its high banks, or *rivo alto*, which formed a dry and easily defended redoubt amid the marsh and mud of the lagoon. While San Marco developed into the city's political heart, the Rivoaltus became its commercial hub, where all manner of staple and exotic goods were traded in the "Bazaar of Europe."

LA PADOVANA

This leather store pulls in locals and visitors, all attracted by the classic, middle-range shoes, boots and accessories for men and women. They are not at fashion's cutting-edge but well made and you'll find seasonal numbers.

✚ J6 ✉ SS Filippo e Giacomo, Castello 4272 ☎ 041 522 4106 🚊 San Zaccaria 1, 2

PANTAGRUELICA

Pantagruelica is arguably one of the finest food shops in Venice, offering the best produce from all over Italy, including a great selection of local wines. The emphasis is on quality, with plenty of organic produce. The enthusiastic owner is always happy to spend time talking about the food producers he patronizes.

✚ E6 ✉ Campo San Barnaba, Dorsoduro 2844 ☎ 041 523 6766 🚊 Ca' Rezzonico 1

IL PAPIRO

A fine little shop, with branches around the world, selling marbled paper as well as handsome desk objects, cards, notebooks, diaries and other pretty stationery. There are two other outlets in the city.

✚ G6 ✉ Calle del Piovan, San Marco 2764 ☎ 041 523 5126 🚊 Giglio 1

PAULY
pauly.it

Pauly has been selling the finest Venetian glass since 1866. Its warren of showrooms contain all manner of treasures. There is also an outlet on the Piazza San Marco.

✚ G3 ✉ Ponte Consorz Calle Largo, Castello 4391 ☎ 041 520 9899 🚊 All services to San Zaccaria

PELLETERIA MARIA

There's a huge range of leather bags, wallets and purses here, all made in Italy and all at excellent prices. Designs and colors change as fashions come and go, but they always stock a good selection of classic bags both large and small.

🇬 G6 ✉ Calle Spezier, San Marco 2630 ☎ 041 523 7814 🚤 Giglio 1

PIED À TERRE

piedaterre-venice.com

This tiny shop, behind the market stalls at the foot of the Rialto bridge, has the best selection in Venice of *friulani*, lovely velvet slippers that come in myriad jewel-bright colors, with non-slip soles made of recycled bicycle tyres—comfortable, hard-wearing and quintessentially Venetian.

🇭 H4 ✉ Ruga d'Orefici, 60 Rialto/San Polo 60 ☎ 041 528 5513 🚤 Rialto Mercato 1

TRAGICOMICA

tragicomica.it

Superb handmade masks, created by an artist trained at Venice's Accademia delle Belle Arti, echo the 18th-century heyday of *Carnevale*. Look for Harlequins, Columbines and pantaloons, the plague doctor and some imaginative mythological masks.

🇫 F5 ✉ Calle dei Nomboli, San Polo 2800 ☎ 041 721 102 🚤 San Tomà N, 1, 2

SOUVENIRS

If you are hoping to take home some glass from Murano but have no time to visit try Marina & Susanna Sent (▷ 127). If there's no time to take a trip to Burano but lace is your thing there are some lovely examples at Annelie in the Calle Lunga Santa Barbara in Dorsoduro, selling tablecloths, sheets and bed clothes at affordable prices.

VENETIA STUDIUM

venetiastudium.com

Inspired by Fortuny, this beautiful store offers sumptuous lamps, textiles and accessories, in fabrics ranging from richly colored figured velvet and damask to silk and satin, while the lamps are based on the original designs. It's not cheap, but a clutch bag, scarf or pillow makes the perfect Venetian souvenir.

🇬 G7 ✉ Calle del Bastion, Dorsoduro 180/a ☎ 041 523 6935 🚤 Salute 1 or Accademia 1, 2

ZAZÙ

Fabrics are natural and the cut is beautiful, with items such as draped tops, voluminous trousers tapering at the ankle and bias-cut skirts in softest jersey, all style trademarks. Strong colors are used alongside grey and black, or tones of sand and off-white.

🇫 F5 ✉ Calle dei Saoneri, San Polo 2750 ☎ 041 715 426 🚤 San Tomà 1, 2

SHOP

PRACTICALITIES

Food shops and bakeries are usually open 8.30–1 and 4–7, though virtually all close on Wednesday afternoon and Sunday. For locals, mornings are set aside for food shopping and this is the time to visit the city's markets at the Rialto and the locality, which open around 8.30. Food served by weight (including bread) is sold by the *chilo*, *mezzo chilo* (kilo and half-kilo; about 2lb and 1lb) and, more commonly, by the *etto* (100g; about 4oz), plural *etti*. Supermarkets are open daily, normally from 8–8.

Entertainment

Once you've done with sightseeing for the day, you'll find lots of other great things to do with your time in this chapter, even if all you want to do is relax with a drink. In this section establishments are listed alphabetically.

ENTERTAINMENT

Introduction

If Venice is beautiful beyond words by day, at night it's possibly lovelier still. With the day trippers gone, most streets and alleys away from the main squares are eerily quiet, perfect for a late stroll in the velvet summer darkness.

Night-time Enchantment

Most visitors to Venice have only a few nights to enjoy the city's night-time atmosphere, and there's no better way to do so than take a walk off the beaten track. Venice is one of the safest cities in the world, so you should have no worries about exploring its dark streets. Wherever you go, you'll find yourself ambling through an atmospheric world of medieval corners and narrow streets that open up to views enhanced by the combination of darkness and artificial light. Moonlight glistens on the water and the only sounds are distant, echoing footsteps and the slap of water on stone–magical indeed. Round it off with a nightcap or copy the natives and buy a *gelato* (ice cream) to enjoy as you go.

What's On

All very well for a few nights, but the evening may come when you're looking for entertainment. It has to be said the choice is limited, and you won't find clubs, pubs and thumping music: Venice goes to bed

DARK WATERS

Few things are more enchanting than a trip down the Canal Grande under a starlit sky. Indeed, it is almost worth organizing your arrival in the city for nightfall, so that you can approach your hotel by *vaporetto* or water taxi under the cover of darkness: It may be the most memorable part of your trip. And if you are going to lavish a small fortune on a gondola ride, make sure it is at night. Better still, take it in the silent, dark-dappled canals away from the main waterways.

Clockwise from top: Live music entertains patrons of Caffè Florian; the Canal Grande; a couple standing near fairy lights on a canal bridge; viewing artists' work on

remarkably early. Scattered throughout the city, though, are late-night bars, many with live music at least two or three times a week, and a handful of clubs. Follow the students to Campo Santa Margherita, where there's plenty of late music, or head to northern Cannaregio, where the Fondamenta della Misericordia has a string of late-opening bars. For something a bit more elegant, you could hit the tables at the Casino, housed right on the Canal Grande in a stunning *palazzo*.

The Cultural Scene

Many visitors take advantage of Venice's cultural life, surprisingly vibrant for what is, in essence, a small provincial city. There are concerts of Venetian music virtually every evening somewhere in the city, many featuring performers dressed in 18th-century costumes playing Vivaldi against the backdrop of some beautiful *salone* in a sumptuous *palazzo*. The opera season at the wonderful Fenice runs from September until June, and city theaters often stage concerts and occasional dance performances.

To see what's on while you're there, pick up a copy of the day-by-day listings magazine, *Un Ospite di Venezia*, published monthly and available from tourist information offices and some hotels.

ENTERTAINMENT

VALUE FOR MONEY

If you're watching the budget, you can have a great-value evening by taking a *vaporetto* trip up or down the Canal Grande and alighting at San Marco or the Accademia. From San Marco you can stroll along the Riva degli Schiavoni, with its fabulous evening views, while the Accademia stop gives access to the Zattere, a sheltered quayside with views to the Giudecca, benches and Nico (▷ 149), one of the best *gelaterie*. Other options include taking a picnic to the Lido, window-shopping in the upmarket streets of San Marco, or great people-watching.

Piazza San Marco; Basilica di San Marco illuminated in the dark; a night-time view from Ponte dell'Accademia

Directory

San Marco

Live Entertainment
Venezia the Show
Music Clubs and Bars
Bacaro Jazz
Torino@Notte
Vino Vino
Theater, Opera and Classical Music
Musica in Palazzo
Teatro La Fenice

Cannaregio

Live Entertainment
Casinò Municipale di Venezia
Music Clubs and Bars
Algiubagio
Paradiso Perduto
Zenevia
Theater, Opera and Classical Music
Teatro Fondamenta Nuove
Teatro Malibran
Cinema
Cinema Multisala Giorgione Movie D'Essai

Castello

Music Clubs and Bars
Giorgione

Theater, Opera and Classical Music
Fondazione Querini Stampalia

San Polo and Santa Croce

Cinema
Arena di Campo San Polo
Music Clubs and Bars
Bagolo
Caffè dei Frari
Do Mori
Theater, Opera and Classical Music
Chiesa di San Giacometto
Palazzetto Bru Zane
Santa Maria Gloriosa dei Frari
Scuola Grande di San Giovanni Evangelista

Dorsoduro

Music Clubs and Bars
Cantina del Vino già Schiavi
Orange
Piccolo Mondo
Round Midnight
Suzie Café
Venice Jazz Club
Theater, Opera and Classical Music
Santa Maria della Salute

Entertainment A–Z

ALGIUBAGIO

algiubagio.net
Right by the *vaporetto* landing stage, this busy, modern and welcoming bar is a good place for a warming or reviving drink and snack while waiting for, or after disembarking from, a boat. Or drop by during a stroll around the farther reaches of Cannaregio.

🔲 J3 ✉ Fondamenta Nuove, Cannaregio 5039 ☎ 041 523 6084 🕒 Wed–Mon 7am–midnight 🚤 Fondamente Nove 4.1, 4.2, 5.1, 5.2, 12, 13, 21, 22

ARENA DI CAMPO SAN POLO

For six weeks from late July to early September this large *campo* is transformed into an open-air cinema, attracting audiences of up

ENTERTAINMENT

to 1,000 people. The backdrop of flickering hues across crumbling Venetian buildings adds to the drama. Films, mainstream and festival hits, are usually dubbed into Italian.

🏛 F5 ✉ Campo San Polo, San Polo ☎ 041 524 1320 🕐 Phone for latest details 🚤 San Silvestro 1, San Tomà N, 1, 2

BACARO JAZZ

bacarojazz.com

The fabulous Cuban *barista* (barman) here does his utmost to make you feel welcome, and more importantly mixes a mean *mojito*. Expect plenty of jazz and *gondolieri* enjoying themselves. There is good food, too.

🏛 H5 ✉ Salizzada del Fontego dei Tedeschi, San Marco 5546 ☎ 041 528 5249 🕐 Daily 11am–2am 🚤 Rialto N, 1, 2

BAGOLO

Located on a pretty and tucked-away square with small cafés, bars and restaurants, Bagolo is an atmospheric place to drink, particularly with its low lighting and candlelit tables out on the *campo* in summer.

🏛 F4 ✉ Campo San Giacomo dell'Orio, Santa Croce 1584 ☎ 041 717 584 🕐 Tue–Sun 8am–11pm 🚤 Riva de Biasio 1, 5.1, 5.2

CAFFÈ DEI FRARI

This is a great place for an aperitif, especially if you want to dine nearby. Many Venetians start their night with the house spritz or a glass of Prosecco.

🏛 F5 ✉ Fondamenta dei Frari, San Polo 2564 ☎ 041 524 1877 🕐 Daily 8am–9pm. Closed 15 days in Aug 🚤 San Tomà N, 1, 2

CANTINA DEL VINO GIÀ SCHIAVI

cantinaschiavi.com

Here is an old-fashioned wine bar that really looks the part, set almost opposite San Trovaso and one of Venice's few remaining gondola workshops.

🏛 E7 ✉ Fondamenta Nani-Meravegie, Dorsoduro 992 ☎ 041 523 0034 🕐 Closed Sun pm 🚤 Accademia or Zattere N, 1, 2, 6, 8

CASINÒ MUNICIPALE DI VENEZIA

casinovenezia.it

Venice's popular Casinò Municipale (Municipal Casino), one of only a handful in Italy, is housed in the impressive Palazzo Vendramin-Calergi. Dress code is smart—a jacket and tie for men. Guests must be over age 18 and bring ID.

🏛 F3 ✉ Palazzo Vendramin-Calergi, Calle Larga Vendramin, off Rio Terrà della Maddalena, Cannaregio 2040 ☎ 041 529 7111 🕐 Daily 2.45pm–2.30am 🚤 San Marcuola N, 1, 2 💰 Expensive

CHIESA DI SAN GIACOMETTO

This intimate church of San Giacomo di Rialto, affectionately

---

EVENING PASTIMES

Venice does not have the nightlife to match other major cities. For many Venetians an evening out consists of a meal or drink with friends rounded off with a stroll to a bar for a coffee or ice cream. One of the best places to join them is in squares such as Campo San Polo (🏛 F5). *Scuole* and churches are also popular for classical music concerts.

known as San Giacometto, near the Rialto markets, is considered to be the oldest in Venice. It hosts concerts by the Ensemble Antonio Vivaldi and other guest orchestras.

🟦 H4 ✉ Campo di San Giacometto, San Polo 30125 ☎ 041 426 6559 🕐 Phone for times 🚤 Rialto, San Silvestro 1

CINEMA MULTISALA GIORGIONE MOVIE D'ESSAI

A good selection of art-house films is shown at this two-screen Cannaregio cinema. Hollywood films are often dubbed into Italian.

🟦 H4 ✉ Rio Terrà dei Franceschi, Cannaregio 4612 ☎ 041 522 6298 🕐 Phone for latest details 🚤 Ca' d'Oro N, 1

DO MORI

The most authentic and atmospheric of Venice's old-time *bacari* (▷ panel; below) has been in business since 1462. It's always bustling with people from the nearby Rialto markets. It serves good snacks and stocks 350 wines. All guests must stand.

🟦 G4 ✉ Calle do Mori, off Ruga Vecchia San Giovanni, San Polo 429 ☎ 041 522 5401 🕐 Mon–Sat 8.30–8.30 🚤 Rialto N, 1, 2

FONDAZIONE QUERINI STAMPALIA

querinistampalia.it

This cultural institution organizes a diverse selection of artistic events,

with regular Friday and Saturday classical concerts held in the opulent surroundings of a 15th-century *palazzo salone*.

🟦 J5 ✉ Campiello Querini Stampalia, Castello 5252 ☎ 041 271 1411 🕐 Hours vary 🚤 Rialto N, 1, 2 and all services to San Zaccaria

GIORGIONE

ristorantegiorgione.it

Venetians flock to this trattoria-cum-pizzeria for the quality food, Friulian wines and Venetian folk music. The owner, Lucio Bisutto, is one of the art's leading exponents and frequently performs his all-singing and a little dancing "fisherman's tales."

🟦 M7 ✉ Via Giuseppe Garibaldi, Castello 1533 ☎ 041 522 8727 🕐 Closed Wed 🚤 Giardini N, 1, 4.1, 4.2, 5.1, 5.2

MUSICA IN PALAZZO

musicapalazzo.com

Watch grand opera on a chamber music scale in the evocative surroundings of the 18th-century Palazzo Barbarigo Minotto. Performances of some best-loved operas, such as *La Traviata* and *The Barber of Seville*, take place in the state rooms of the *palazzo*, with performers singing their roles among the audience.

🟦 G7 ✉ Palazzo Barbarigo Minotto, Fondamenta Barbarigo, San Marco 2504 ☎ 39 340 971 7272 🕐 Peformances daily 8.30pm 🚤 Giglio 1

WINE BARS

Old-fashioned wine bars, or *bacari,* are a Venetian way of life. One of the city's more civilized habits is the custom of breaking up the day with an *ombra* ("shadow"), a small glass of wine that takes its name from the idea of escaping the heat of the sun for a restorative tipple. A small snack, or *cichetto,* usually accompanies the drink. An *enoteca* is a more refined bar, with a greater choice of wines and a range of reasonably priced meals.

ORANGE

orangebar.it

Orange spritz is the signature drink here in this orange-themed bar, restaurant and champagne lounge. There's an upstairs terrace where you can watch life on the Campo, but most of the achingly chic drinkers are too busy watching each other.

➕ E6 ✉ Campo Santa Margherita, Dorsoduro 3054/a ☎ 041 523 4740 🕐 Daily 8am–2am ⛴ Ca' Rezzonico 1

PALAZZETTO BRU ZANE

bru-zane.com

The Palazzetto Bru Zane opened in 2008 as the venue for around 100 concerts annually, all themed to aspects of the 19th-century French Romantic movement, either a composer, a specific instrument or a musical theme. This is a good contrast to Venice's staple musical diet of 18th-century Italian offerings. Some concerts are given in the Scuola Grande di San Rocco.

➕ E4 ✉ Calle dell'Ogio, San Polo 2368 ☎ 041 521 1005 🕐 Telephone or check website for times and schedules ⛴ San Tomà, Piazzale Roma

PARADISO PERDUTO

ilparadisoperduto.wordpress.com

The atmosphere at this renowned nightspot makes up for the fairly average food that is served here. The inexpensive wine and eclectic music attract a diverse, alternative crowd, and its legendary all-night theme parties have ruffled many locals' feathers over the years.

➕ G2 ✉ Fondamenta della Misericordia, Cannaregio 2640 ☎ 041 720 581 🕐 Tue–Sun 11–3, 6–2 ⛴ Madonna dell'Orto 4.1, 4.2, 5.1, 5.2

CARNEVALE

Venice's famous carnival takes its name from the Latin *carnem levare*, or *carne vale*—the "farewell to meat." It probably began in the city's 15th-century private clubs. Resurrected in 1979 (by a group of non-Venetians), it emulates the great pre-Lenten festivals of the 18th century: Thousands of tourists dressing in masks and extravagant costumes to indulge in a series of events. Today, the carnival lasts just 10 days (up to the beginning of Lent).

PICCOLO MONDO

piccolomondo.biz

This may not be the most hip, and it is probably the smallest, but Piccolo Mondo is one of Venice's few nightclubs.

➕ F7 ✉ Calle Contarini Corfù, Dorsoduro 1056/a ☎ 041 520 0371 🕐 Tue–Sun 11pm–4am ⛴ Accademia N, 1, 2

ROUND MIDNIGHT

This intimate club attracts all sorts for the mainstream music. They feature occasional live acts, which are popular with students.

➕ E6 ✉ Calle dei Pugli, off Fondamenta dello Squero, Dorsoduro 3102 ☎ 041 523 2056 🕐 Mon, Wed–Sat 10pm–4am ⛴ Ca' Rezzonico 1

SANTA MARIA GLORIOSA DEI FRARI

chorusvenezia.org

basilicadeifrari.it

There are sacred music concert series in spring and autumn, sometimes featuring orchestral ensembles, other times organ recitals. The church makes a great setting for music.

➕ E5 ✉ Campo dei Frari, San Polo ☎ 041 522 2637 🕐 Phone for latest details ⛴ San Tomà N, 1, 2

Bright lights in Riva degli Schiavoni

SANTA MARIA DELLA SALUTE

This is the venue for a variety of classical organ music. As well as performances by the lead organist of the basilica, guest performers also appear as part of Sunday Mass at 11am every week.

➕ G7 ✉ Campo della Salute, Dorsoduro 1 ☎ 041 522 5558 🕐 Phone for latest details 🚤 Salute 1

SCUOLA GRANDE DI SAN GIOVANNI EVANGELISTA

prgroup.netsons.org

The stunning main hall of this important Scuola Grande is the backdrop for spring and autumn performances of some of Italy's best-loved operas. Book online or buy your tickets at the door.

➕ E5 ✉ Campiello della Scuola, San Polo 2454 ☎ 041 426 6559 🕐 Feb–May, Sep–Oct; telephone or check website for times and schedules 🚤 San Tomà, Piazzale Roma

SUZIE CAFÉ

Popular with students in the day, this place transforms into a swinging bar at night. On Friday nights live jazz groups, or reggae and funk bands perform.

➕ D7 ✉ Campo San Basegio, Dorsoduro 1527A–B ☎ 041 522 7502 🕐 Mon–Thu 7–7, Fri–Sat 8am–1am (if there's a concert in the *campo*) 🚤 Zattere N, 1, 2, 5.1, 5.2, 6, 8

TEATRO LA FENICE

teatrolafenice.it

This famous opera house (▷ 75) hosts a full schedule of operas and other concerts, and you can also join a daytime tour to see the fabulous interior.

➕ G6 ✉ Campo San Fantin, San Marco 1965 ☎ 041 786 500; information 041 2424 or 041 786 511; for tickets fenice.artacom.it/biglietteria 🚤 Giglio 1

TEATRO FONDAMENTA NUOVE

teatrofondamentanuove.it

Venice's premier avant-garde venue, set on the northern lagoon in remote Cannaregio, was founded in 1993 in an old joiners' shop. Teatro Fondamenta Nuove stages contemporary dance and organizes performances, film festivals, workshops and exhibitions as part of its innovative Art and Technology project, which explores the relationship between artistic creativity and technology.

WHAT'S ON

Details of films, concerts and exhibitions in Venice are listed in the *Spettacoli* section of daily editions of local newspapers such as *Il Gazzettino* and *La Nuova Venezia*. *Un Ospite di Venezia*, a free Italian/English magazine available from hotels and tourist offices, also contains detailed listings (published weekly in peak season, monthly during the off season). Tourist offices always have plenty of posters and leaflets on current events (▷ 133). Also keep an eye open for posters on the streets.

➕ J3 ✉ Fondamente Nuove, Cannaregio 5013 ☎ 041 522 4498 🕐 Phone for latest details ⛴ Fondamente Nove N, 1, 4.1, 4.2, 5.1, 5.2, 13, 21, 22

TEATRO MALIBRAN

teatrolafenice.it

A theater has stood on this site since 1677, and the Teatro Malibran was Venice's most elite performance venue throughout the 18th century. Today it stages well-known operas such as *La Traviata* and more modern works, as well as occasional Shakespeare plays in Italian, classical concerts and first-class ballet productions.

➕ H4 ✉ Calle dei Milion, Cannaregio 5873 ☎ 041 786 603; box office 041 786 601 🕐 Phone for latest details ⛴ Rialto N, 1, 2

TORINO@NOTTE

Live jazz, beer, spritz and toasted sandwiches make up the staple diet of the fun-loving crowd here. The action spills out onto the *campo* during the summer and during Carnival.

➕ H5 ✉ Campo San Luca, San Marco 459 ☎ 041 522 3914 🕐 Tue–Sat 7.30pm–1am ⛴ Rialto N, 1, 2

VENEZIA THE SHOW

teatrosangallo.net

If you want an entertaining look at the history of Venice, the nightly shows here combine live action with state-of-the-art video, music and sound presentations to evoke the history of the city and the atmosphere of Carnival—touristy, but good fun.

➕ H6 ✉ Campo San Gallo, San Marco 1097 ☎ 041 241 2002 🕐 Performances daily 7pm ⛴ San Marco Vallaresso, San Marco Giardinetti 1, 2 💶 Expensive

VENICE JAZZ CLUB

venicejazzclub.com

The VJC quartet, made up of piano, drums, double bass and guitar, is a passionate group of experienced jazz artists who play standards and revisit modern compositions; they have frequent guest artists too.

➕ E6 ✉ Ponte dei Pugni, Dorsoduro 3102 ☎ 340 150 4985 🕐 Mon–Wed, Fri–Sat 7pm–11pm ⛴ Ca' Rezzonico 1

VINO VINO

vinovinowinebar.com

Rather more showy and smarter than some of Venice's humbler bars, this two-roomed spot close to the opera house has more than 100 different wines to accompany its snacks and meals.

➕ G6 ✉ Ponte delle Veste, Calle delle Veste, San Marco 2007a ☎ 041 241 7688 🕐 Daily 11.30–11.30 ⛴ Giglio 1

ZENEVIA

This bar is popular for its intimate nooks inside and its seating outside on Campo Santa Maria Formosa. There is occasional live music.

➕ J5 ✉ Campo Santa Maria Formosa, Cannaregio 5548 ☎ 041 520 6266 🕐 Wed–Mon 9pm–2am ⛴ Zattere, Rialto

WHERE TO GO

Nightlife in Venice is decidedly low key. Late-night possibilities are really limited to bars and live-music cafés, where you can hear jazz, blues or reggae, with the occasional Latino or rock session. A main party area is Fondementa della Misericordia in Cannaregio, where a string of waterfront bars and tiny clubs transforms the whole quayside into one long nightspot.

Eat

There are places to eat across the city to suit all tastes and budgets. In this section establishments are listed alphabetically.

EAT

Introduction

Venetian cooking is as individual as the city, with the accent on fish and seafood, as well as meat, game and vegetables from the lagoon islands, and rice, polenta and pasta dishes. Avoid places offering a *menu turistico*, and expect prices to be high.

When to Eat
Breakfast is usually served between 8 and 10. Locals often pop into a bar on their way to work for a cappuccino and a *briosc* (pastry). Venetian restaurants popular with locals operate two timescales—one for them and one for visitors. Working Venetians eat lunch between 12 and 1 and dinner between 8 and 9. Restaurants aimed mainly at tourists start lunch at 12.30 and dinner at 7, though some serve throughout the day.

Where to Eat
Like many Italian cities, there is a confusing array of eating places. A *ristorante* tends to be expensive, whereas the trattoria is less formal, less expensive, and often family-run. Such places may not have a printed menu, and the waiter will reel off a list of what's on offer; many speak enough English to help you choose. *Osterie* were basic, and some still are, but the term is often synonymous with good food and rustic elegance. *Pizzerie* in Venice tend to open all day; ovens are electric so Venetian *pizze* aren't as good as in Rome or Naples.

WHAT TO EAT

A full Venetian meal is gargantuan—*antipasti,* a *primo* (first course) of soup, rice or pasta, a *secondo* (main course) of fish with vegetable *contorni* (side dishes), then *formaggi* (cheese) and *dolce* (pudding). Do as the locals do and pick and mix. Few Venetians eat either cheese or pudding in restaurants, preferring to head for a *pasticceria* or choose a *gelato* (ice cream) if they want something sweet to round off a meal.

From the top: Caffè Florian; fritelle (small doughnuts) are a popular snack; outdoor tables at Caffè Florian; Osteria la Zucca

EAT

Directory

San Marco

Cafés and Bars
Caffè Florian
Teamo
Fine Dining
Harry's Bar
Fish and Seafood
Acquapazza
Al Conte Pescaor
Ice Cream
Paolin
Trattorie* and *Osterie
Osteria al Bacareto
Osteria ai Rusteghe

Cannaregio

Trattorie* and *Osterie
Osteria l'Orto dei Mori
Venetian
Anice Stellato
Trattoria Cea
Vini Da Gigio

Castello

Fish and Seafood
Al Mascaron
Corte Sconta
Trattorie* and *Osterie
Alla Rivetta
Da Remigio
Osteria alle Testiere
Osteria Oliva Nera

San Polo and Santa Croce

Cafés and Bars
Bottega del Caffè Dersut
Ciak
Fine Dining
Poste Vecie
Fish and Seafood
Da Ignazio
Italian
Antica Birraria la Corte

Pizzerie
Alle Oche
Muro Venezia Frari
Il Refolo
Trattorie* and *Osterie
Osteria la Zucca
Trattoria San Tomà
Venetian
Alla Madonna
Antiche Carampane
Bancogiro
Ribó

Dorsoduro

Cafés and Bars
Improntacafe
Fine Dining
Antica Locanda Montin
Ice Cream
GROM
Nico
Pizzerie
Casin dei Nobili
Venetian
La Bitta
Dona Onesta
Taverna San Trovaso

EAT

Eating A–Z

PRICES

Prices are approximate, based on a 3-course meal for one person.

€€€	over €55
€€	€35–€55
€	under €35

ACQUAPAZZA €€–€€€

veniceacquapazza.com

The accent is mainly on fish: Starters include prawns and rocket with balsamic dressing and a seafood platter; follow with the catch of the day or a fish risotto.

➕ G6 ✉ Campo Sant'Angelo, San Marco 3808 ☎ 041 277 0688 🕐 Tue–Sun lunch and dinner. Closed Mon and Jan 🚤 Sant'Angelo

AL CONTE PESCAOR €€

alcontepescaor.it

A wonderful tiny fish restaurant that caters to Venetians, despite its proximity to Piazza San Marco.

➕ J6–H6 ✉ Piscina San Zulian, San Marco 544 ☎ 041 522 1483 🕐 Mon–Sat lunch and dinner. Closed Sun and Jan in winter 🚤 San Marco Vallaresso, San Marco Giardinetti N, 1, 2

AL MASCARON €€

osteriamascaron.it

This nice old bar-trattoria has a brisk, informal atmosphere, a beamed ceiling and black-and-white photos on the walls. Fish and seafood is served, and it is so popular (reservations essential) that the owners have opened Alla Mascareta for wine and snacks at No. 5183.

➕ J5 ✉ Calle Lunga Santa Maria Formosa, Castello 5525 ☎ 041 522 5995 🕐 Mon–Sat lunch and dinner. Closed Sun and mid-Dec to mid-Jan 🚤 Rialto N, 1, 2

ALLA MADONNA €€

ristoranteallamadonna.com

One of the most authentic and one of the oldest restaurants in the city, Alla Madonna has the look of a Venetian restaurant of 30 years ago. It is popular for business meetings and family celebrations. The food is rigorously Venetian.

➕ H5 ✉ Calle della Madonna, San Polo 594 ☎ 041 522 3824 🕐 Thu–Tue lunch and dinner. Closed Wed and 2 weeks in Aug 🚤 Rialto N, 1, 2

ALLA RIVETTA €€

An inexpensive but good small trattoria close to Piazza San Marco that makes a pleasant alternative to some of the more expensive places. It is often very busy.

➕ J6 ✉ Ponte San Provolo, near Campo SS Filippo e Giacomo, Castello 4625 ☎ 041 528 7302 🕐 Tue–Sun lunch and dinner. Closed Mon and Aug 🚤 All services to San Zaccaria

---

WINES

Most of Venice's wine comes from the Veneto region on the mainland. Its best-known wines are the usually unexceptional Soave (white), and Valpolicella and Bardolino (reds). More interesting whites include Soave Classico, Bianco di Custoza, Tocai, Pinot Grigio and the wines of the Breganze region. The best white of all is Prosecco, a delicious dry sparkling wine often drunk as an aperitif. Interesting reds include Raboso, the wines of the Colle Berici and Lison-Pramaggiore regions, and two excellent dessert wines: Amarone and Recioto della Valpolicella.

Caffè Florian

Fish, such as this turbot, and seafood are superb in Venice

ALLE OCHE €–€€

Usually heaving with students, this lively pizzeria serves thin, crisp *pizze* with a huge range of toppings and a few pastas dishes. There are some tables outside.

➕ F4 ✉ Calle del Tintor, San Polo 1552 ☎ 041 524 1161 ⏱ Daily lunch and dinner 🚢 Riva di Biasio 1

ANICE STELLATO €€

osterianicestellato.com

The "Star Anise" combines its role as a down-to-earth neighborhood *bacaro* (wine bar) with that of a rustically elegant trattoria serving traditional Venetian food. You may find the bar area packed with locals but, once you have found a table, you can enjoy a delicious meal, its dishes entirely dependent on the season and what's available in the market. For a light lunch, choose saucers of *cichetti* (snacks), with *ombra*, a glass of local white wine.

➕ F2 ✉ Fondamenta della Sensa, Cannaregio 3272 ☎ 041 720 744 ⏱ Wed–Mon lunch and dinner. Tue dinner only 🚢 Sant'Alvise 4.1, 4.2, 5.1, 5.2

ANTICA BIRRARIA LA CORTE €€

birrarialacorte.it

This converted warehouse is one of a new breed of Venetian restaurants. The seating spills out into evocative Campo San Polo, making it perfect for sunny days and balmy evenings. The inside is contemporary, with clean lines and chrome. The food nods to all the Venetian and Italian classics—it's good quality. You can snack or go the whole hog here.

➕ F5 ✉ Campo San Polo, San Polo 2168 ☎ 041 275 0570 ⏱ Daily 10am–midnight; kitchen 12–3, 6–10.30 🚢 San Silvestro 1

ANTICA LOCANDA MONTIN €€

locandamontin.com

This venerable restaurant, not far from the Gallerie dell'Accademia, has been famous for decades and is popular with the rich and famous, although today it does depend somewhat on its former reputation. The quality of food is now once again touching former heights; eat in the painting-lined dining room or on the shaded outside terrace to the rear.

E7 ✉ Fondamenta di Borgo, Dorsoduro 1147 ☎ 041 522 7151 🕐 Tue dinner, Thu–Mon lunch and dinner. Closed Wed 🚤 Zattere or Ca' Rezzonico N, 1, 2, 5.1, 5.2, 6, 8

ANTICHE CARAMPANE €€€
veneziaristoranti.it

One of the association of Buona Accoglienza restaurants, whose members aim to promote traditional Venetian cooking and hospitality, this off-the-beaten-track restaurant specializes in beautifully cooked, elegantly served seafood and fish. The style is a modern take on tradition, seen at its best in dishes such as *spaghetti alla granseola* (spaghetti with spider crab), *cassopipa* (pasta with a spicy fish sauce) or *branzino in salsa di peperoni* (sea bass in sweet pepper sauce). The wine list is long, desserts elegant and imaginative. Booking is essential.

G4 ✉ Ponte delle Tette, San Polo 1911 ☎ 041 524 0165 🕐 Tue–Sat lunch and dinner. Closed Sun, Mon 🚤 San Stae/Rialto Mercato

BANCOGIRO €€
osteriabancogiro.it

Housed in one of the 16th-century buildings around the markets, the Bancogiro is a welcoming restaurant that doubles as a bar serving *cichetti*. The menu relies on local, seasonal ingredients, prepared with a modern twist by chef Jacopo Zamboni. The brick-vaulted interior is understated and elegant, and the outside tables are set right beside the Canal Grande.

H4 ✉ San Giacometto, San Polo 1220 ☎ 41 523 2061 🕐 Tue–Sun 9am–midnight. Closed Mon 🚤 Rialto Mercato 1

LA BITTA €€

There's no fish on the menu here, but the meat is farm-sourced, and it's one of the best places to sample *fegato alla veneziana*, the classic Venetian liver and onions served with creamy polenta.

E6 ✉ Calle Lunga San Barnaba, Dorsoduro 2753/a ☎ 041 523 0531 🕐 Mon–Sat dinner. Closed Sun 🚤 Ca' Rezzonico 1

BOTTEGA DEL CAFFÈ DERSUT €

Huge windows allow a glimpse into the interior of this popular café, where you can stand at the bar or relax on one of the deep sofas while you enjoy a speciality coffee—different flavors, different toppings, many laced with cream—or get a vitamin fix in the form of a blended veggie juice or mixed fruit smoothie made to order. They also serve pastries, tarts and cakes.

E5 ✉ Campo dei Frari, San Polo 3014 ☎ 041 303 2159 🕐 Daily breakfast, snacks all day 🚤 San Tomà

HARRY'S BAR

This famous bar and restaurant was founded in 1931 when, according to legend, a now-forgotten American ("Harry") remarked to hotel barman Giuseppe Cipriani that Venice lacked for nothing except a good bar. The enterprising Cipriani duly sought financial backing, found an old rope store near Piazza San Marco, and Harry's Bar was born. It is now a place of high prices, good food and great cocktails, and—in the words of writer Gore Vidal—"a babble of barbaric voices...the only place for Americans in acute distress to go for comfort and advice...".

EAT

CAFFÈ FLORIAN €–€€€

caffeflorian.com

The oldest, prettiest and most expensive of Venice's famous cafés has been serving customers since 1720. It was once favored by Lord Byron and the German poet Goethe. Prices are high, but treat yourself for the experience and the chance to admire the interior.

✚ H6 ✉ Piazza San Marco, San Marco 56–59 ☎ 041 520 5641 🕐 Daily 9am–midnight breakfast, light lunch, snacks all day 🚋 San Marco Vallaresso, San Marco Giardinetti N, 1, 2

CASIN DEI NOBILI €–€€

There's the attraction of a buzzing student atmosphere and eating outside in the pretty garden in summer at this bustling pizzeria cum restaurant. The menu features all the solid Venetian classics, but, if you're watching the pennies, pizza is the best bet.

✚ E6 ✉ Sottoportego del Casin dei Nobili, Dorsoduro 2765 ☎ 041 241 1841 🕐 Tue–Sun 12–10.30. Closed Mon 🚋 Ca' Rezzonico 1

CIAK €

A pleasant, relaxed bar, used by everyone from gondoliers to society ladies to adjourn to after visiting Santa Maria Gloriosa dei Frari and the Scuola Grande di San Rocco. They do good lunchtime snacks and sandwiches.

✚ F5 ✉ Campiello San Tomà, San Polo 2807 ☎ 041 528 5150 🕐 Daily breakfast, snacks all day 🚋 San Tomà N, 1, 2

CORTE SCONTA €€

veneziaristoranti.it

Many Venetians and visitors alike rate the popular Corte Sconta as their preferred restaurant, despite

its slightly peripheral location. Fairly small and always busy, the cooking and seafood are rarely less than excellent. There is no menu, so try to follow waiting staff's recommendations. A garden has tables in summer.

✚ L6 ✉ Calle del Pestrin, Castello 3886 ☎ 041 522 7024 🕐 Tue–Sat lunch and dinner. Closed Sun–Mon 🚋 Arsenale 1, 4.1, 4.2

DA IGNAZIO €€

veneziaristoranti.it

This fairly small, predominantly fish restaurant lies just east of Campo San Tomà, and has the atmosphere of a restaurant from the 1950s. There is a garden for alfresco dining in summer.

✚ F5 ✉ Calle Saoneri, San Polo 2749 ☎ 041 523 4852 🕐 Sun–Fri lunch and dinner. Closed Sat and 3 weeks in Jul and Aug 🚋 San Tomà N, 1, 2

DA REMIGIO €€

Small area *trattorie* are a dying breed in Venice, so this authentic restaurant, despite a redecoration that has removed some old-fashioned touches, is a find. It has just 40 seats, so you will need to reserve or arrive early to share a

EAT

Cherry sorbet and deep-fried custard

table. The food is reliable and homey, pasta and fish are good, and although the wine list is short it is adequate.

🔼 K6 ✉ Salizzada dei Greci, Castello 3416 ☎ 041 523 0089 🕔 Wed–Sun lunch and dinner, Mon dinner. Closed Tue 🚢 Arsenale 1, 4.1, 4.2 or all services to San Zaccaria

DONA ONESTA €€€
donaonesta.it

The "Honest Woman" lives up to its name with fine food at budget prices. It is becoming increasingly well known, however, so try to reserve a table in its single small dining room overlooking a little canal midway between San Pantalon and San Tomà.

🔼 E5 ✉ Calle della Dona Onesta, Dorsoduro 3922 ☎ 041 710 586 🕔 Daily lunch and dinner 🚢 San Tomà N, 1, 2

GROM €
A nationwide chain, GROM has made a big impact with its ices. Flavors change monthly, and nothing is on offer unless it's in season. There is another branch at Strada Nuova (Ca' d'Oro), Cannaregio 3844.

🔼 E6 ✉ San Barnaba, Dorsoduro 2761 ☎ 041 099 1751 🕔 Daily 10–10 🚢 Ca' Rezzonico

HARRY'S BAR €€€
cipriani.com

This legendary establishment is best known for its celebrity status (▷ 146; panel). The restaurant upstairs serves reliable fare, while snacks can be ordered at the downstairs bar. This is *the* place for cocktails—the famous Bellini was invented here.

🔼 H7 ✉ Calle Vallaresso, San Marco 1323 ☎ 041 528 5777 🕔 Lunch and dinner. The bar is open every day but may close during Carnival 🚢 San Marco Vallaresso, San Marco Giardinetti, N, 1, 2

IMPRONTACAFE €–€€
improntacafevenice.com

This part of town is university territory and this lively, modern bar and restaurant, with its late opening hours, pulls in crowds of students and young visitors. You can have breakfast, a light lunch, full dinner or just a drink, and find a buzzy atmosphere. There's a good range of wines by the glass.

MORE OPTIONS

A fixed-price tourist menu *(menù turistico)* usually includes a basic pasta, main course, fruit and half-bottles of wine and water. Food quality is often indifferent—you will probably find many of the same dishes listed on the menu in a budget trattoria as in most expensive restaurants. The difference is primarily in ambience and detail. The *prezzo fisso* (fixed price) menu usually excludes cover, service and beverages. Check what is included in the price.

E5 ✉ Calle dei Preti Crosera,
Dorsoduro 3815 ☎ 041 275 0386
🕐 Mon–Sat breakfast, lunch, dinner and
snacks. Closed Sun 🚤 San Tomà 1, 2

MURO VENEZIA FRARI €–€€

murovenezia.com
Dark wood and minimalist design
bring a feeling of space to this
all-day bar-cum-eatery, where the
menu offers a good range of *pizze*
as well as standard Italian and
Venetian dishes.
F5 ✉ Rio Tera dei Frari, San Polo
2604b/c ☎ 041 524 5310 🕐 Fri–Wed
lunch and dinner. Closed Thu 🚤 San Tomà

NICO €

Organize a walk in the Dorsoduro
district so that you pass this small
waterfront bar renowned for its
ice cream, in particular a praline
concoction known as *gianduiotto*.
E8 ✉ Zattere ai Gesuati, Dorsoduro
922 ☎ 041 522 5293 🕐 Fri–Wed
breakfast, lunch and snacks. Closed Thu
🚤 Zattere N, 2, 5.1, 5.2, 6, 8

OSTERIA AI RUSTEGHI €

airusteghi.com
Venice is famous for its panini
and *tramezzini* (filled rolls and
sandwiches) and this tiny place
offers well over 30 varieties, which
you can enjoy with a beer or glass
of wine from the long list.
H5 ✉ Campiello del Tintor, San Marco
5513 ☎ 3387 606 034 🕐 Mon–Sat lunch.
Closed Sun 🚤 Rialto 1, 2

OSTERIA AL BACARETO €€

This well-placed traditional trattoria
is in a quiet corner of the city just a
few moments' walk west of the
church of Santo Stefano. You can
have a full meal, snack or a plate
of antipasti with a glass of wine.

F6 ✉ Calle Crosera, San Marco 3447
☎ 041 528 9336 🕐 Mon–Fri lunch and
dinner, Sat lunch. Closed Sun
🚤 Sant'Angelo or San Samuele N, 1, 2

OSTERIA ALLE TESTIERE €€

osterialletestiere.it
One of the top tables in town, if
you can manage to get a reserva-
tion. The food is inexpensive given
the quality that cooking a limited
menu for small numbers allows
the owner to achieve. The focus
is on local dishes, imaginatively
prepared and crammed full of
zinging tastes.
J5 ✉ Calle del Mondo Novo, Castello
5801 ☎ 041 522 7220 🕐 Mon–Sat,
seatings at 7 and 9.15pm 🚤 Rialto N, 1, 2

OSTERIA L'ORTO DEI MORI €€

osteriaortodeimori.com
There aren't many restaurants in
northern Cannaregio, and this is a
hit with both locals and tourists.
The interior looks as if it's been
there for years, with warm
paneling and shining glass, but the
menu is decidedly 21st century,

DRINKS

Venice's water is perfectly safe to drink,
though Venetians prefer mineral water
(acqua minerale)—either sparkling
(gassata) or still *(liscia, naturale* or *non
gassata)*. Bottles come in one litre *(un
litro* or *una bottiglia)* or half-litre *(mezzo
litro* or *mezza bottiglia)* sizes. Bottled fruit
juice is *un succo di frutta*, available in
pear *(pera)*, apricot *(albiccoca)*, peach
(pesca) and other tastes. Fresh juice is
una spremuta, while milkshake is *un frul-
lato*, or *un frappé* if made with ice cream.
Lemon soda is a popular and refreshing
bitter-lemon drink. Ice is *ghiaccio*, and a
slice of lemon is *uno spicchio di limone*.

EAT

with Venetian specialities given a modern twist. Everything is well-sourced, short and seasonal; they refuse to use frozen ingredients.
🔳 G2 ✉ Campo dei Mori, Cannaregio 3386 ☎ 041 524 3677 🕐 Wed–Mon lunch and dinner. Closed Tue 🚤 Orto 4.1, 4.2, 5.1, 5.2

OSTERIA LA ZUCCA €€
lazucca.it

The imaginative and ever-changing food in this pleasantly located *osteria*, especially the vegetable side dishes and main courses, are innovative, at least by Venice's normally conservative standards.
🔳 F4 ✉ Calle del Tintor (or Tentor), Santa Croce 1762 ☎ 041 524 1570 🕐 Mon–Sat lunch and dinner. Closed Sun 🚤 Riva di Biasio 1, 5.1, 5.2

OSTERIA OLIVA NERA €€€
olivanera.com

One of a new breed challenging the old school of Venetian restaurateurs. Its mostly fish and seafood menu shows Venetian cooking can be given a contemporary edge. All fish is fresh from the market. A second restaurant, Oliva Nera II, has opened in the same street at No. 3447 (closed Thursday) offering a more meat-based menu while retaining the same principles of fresh home cooking.
🔳 K6 ✉ Salizzada dei Greci, Castello 3417-18 ☎ 041 522 2170 🕐 Thu–Tue 12–2.30, 7–10 🚤 Services to San Zaccaria

PAOLIN €–€€

The best café in one of Venice's nicest squares has lots of outside tables and very good ice cream.
🔳 F6 ✉ Campo Santo Stefano (Campo Francesco Morosini), San Marco 2962 ☎ 041 522 5576 🕐 Daily breakfast, snacks and ice cream. Closed Dec–Jan 🚤 Accademia N, 1, 2

POSTE VECIE €€€
postevecie.com

Ingredients could hardly be fresher at this appealing fish restaurant, reputedly founded in 1500, alongside the Pescheria fish market. Cooking is refined, but can be variable, and there's a good wine list.
🔳 H4 ✉ Campo della Pescaria, San Polo 1608 ☎ 041 721 822 🕐 Wed–Mon lunch and dinner. Closed Tue and 4 weeks in Jul and Aug 🚤 Rialto N, 1, 2

IL REFOLO €

In a quiet corner near a church, this is popular with locals for good pizzas and a limited selection of pastas and main courses.
🔳 F4 ✉ Campo San Giacomo dell'Olio, Santa Croce 1459 ☎ 041 524 0016 🕐 Tue dinner, Wed–Sun lunch and dinner. Closed Mon and Nov–Mar 🚤 Riva di Biasio or San Stae 1

RIBÓ €€€

This is a refreshingly bright and modern restaurant, serving light and modern Venetian cuisine, and a little off the usual tourist trail.

ETIQUETTE

The procedure when standing up in a bar is to pay for what you want at the cash desk *(la cassa)* and take your receipt *(lo scontrino)* to the bar, where you repeat your order (a tip slapped down on the bar works wonders with the service). Do not then take your drink and sit at an outside table, as you almost always pay a premium to sit down when you order through a waiter. Sitting, a single purchase allows you to relax almost indefinitely.

Expect reasonable (though not inexpensive) prices, superb fresh pasta and fresh fish, and a romantic interior patio garden.

➕ D5 ✉ Fondamenta Minotto, Santa Croce 158 ☎ 041 524 2486 🕐 Tun–Tue lunch and dinner. Closed Wed and 2 weeks in Aug 🚤 San Basilio N, 2, 6, 8

TAVERNA SAN TROVASO €
tavernasantrovaso.it

Not the best cuisine in the city, yet it has reliable cooking and is popular with Venetians. Reserve ahead (especially for Sunday lunch).

➕ E7 ✉ Fondamenta Priuli, Dorsoduro 1016 ☎ 041 520 3703 🕐 Tue–Sun lunch and dinner. Closed Mon 🚤 Accademia N, 1, 2

TEAMO €
teamowinebar.com

This sleek, relaxing, modern wine bar makes a good change of pace from the traditional Venetian snack bar. There's a wide range of *cichetti* at lunch, including both hot and cold fish- or meat-based dishes, or you could try a platter of mixed smoked meats and cheeses.

➕ G6 ✉ Rio Terà della Mandola, San Marco 3795 ☎ 041 528 3787 🕐 Daily lunch and snacks 🚤 Giglio 1

TRATTORIA CEA €–€€
trattoriacea.com

This truly Venetian local eating house has been satisfying the neighborhood for years and you could be the only foreigner in the place. There's a good-value set menu at lunch, or go à la carte and choose from the short menu of mainly fish dishes. If you want to sample *baccalà mantecato* (creamed, dried salt cod), this is the place to try the real thing.

➕ J4 ✉ Campiello Widmann, Cannaregio 5422/a ☎ 041 523 7540 🕐 Mon–Fri lunch and dinner, Sat lunch. Closed Sun 🚤 Fondamente Nove 4.1, 4.2, 5.1, 5.2

TRATTORIA SAN TOMÀ €–€€
trattoriasantoma.com

The pizzas and trattoria food served here are good, but this restaurant's best attraction is its location, only one minute south of Santa Maria Gloriosa dei Frari and the Scuola Grande di San Rocco.

➕ F5 ✉ Campo San Tomà, San Polo 2864 ☎ 041 523 8819 🕐 Summer daily lunch and dinner; winter Wed–Mon lunch and dinner 🚤 San Tomà N, 1, 2

VINI DA GIGIO €€
veneziaristoranti.it

Pretty, relaxed and romantic, this restaurant is on a peaceful canal with two simple beamed rooms and old cabinets. Venetian cooking includes fish and meat dishes, and a short, well-chosen wine list.

➕ G3 ✉ Fondamenta della Chiesa-San Felice, Cannaregio 3628a ☎ 041 528 5140 🕐 Wed–Sun lunch and dinner. Closed Mon and Tue, Jan and 3 weeks in Aug 🚤 Ca' d'Oro N, 1

EAT

Sleep

With options ranging from luxurious to budget hotels, Venice has accommodations to suit everyone. In this section establishments are listed alphabetically.

Introduction

Compared with its population, Venice has more tourist accommodation than any other Italian city. This ranges from 5-star luxury through cutting-edge boutique hotels to low-key, family-run traditional establishments and numerous bed and breakfasts. Despite this, for much of the year Venice remains a seller's market, reflected in the high price of all its accommodation.

What to Expect

Venetian hotels are classified by the Italian state system into five categories from 1- to 5- star (basic to luxury), which reflect facilities rather than room size or decor. Room prices may alter according to the season and all prices must be displayed in the foyer and on the back of bedroom doors; check to see if breakfast is included in this. There are often considerable savings on rack rates by booking online or as part of a package. It's acceptable to ask to see the room; the hotel may have cheaper options than the first room you're shown.

Where to Stay

San Marco has many places to stay and is the heart of the city, but is also very noisy and constantly crowded by day. To the east, Castello is both quieter and cheaper, while to the west Cannaregio has enormous choice, with many budget options near the railway station. Across the Canal Grande, San Polo and Santa Croce have family-run, traditional hotels, particularly around the Rialto, while Dorsoduro, a largely residential area, makes a peaceful choice.

FEELING THE HEAT

Venice is very hot in the summer, so a courtyard or garden is a bonus, as are rooms away from the street. Bear in mind that noise bounces off water and narrow streets, especially if they are major thoroughfares.

From the top: Hotel Palazzo Stern; Accademia-Villa Maravege; detail of a stained-glass window at the Danieli hotel; a red-carpeted staircase in the Danieli

Directory

San Marco

Budget
Fiorita
Mid-Range
Al Piave
Flora

San Polo and Santa Croce

Budget
Ai Due Fanali
Ai Tolentini
Iris
La Villeggiatura

Cannaregio

Mid-Range
Ca' Dogaressa

Castello

Budget
Canada
Doni
Locanda Silva

Mid-Range
Ai Due Principi
Locanda la Corte
Luxury
Danieli

Dorsoduro

Budget
Ca' Foscari
Mid-Range
Accademia-Villa Maravege
Hotel American Dinesen
La Calcina
San Sebastiano Garden
Luxury
Ca' Maria Adele
Centurion Palace
Palazzo Stern

Sleeping A–Z

PRICES	
Prices are approximate and based on a double room for one night.	
€€€€	€501–€800
€€€	€351–€500
€€	€176–€350
€	€90–€175

ACCADEMIA-VILLA MARAVEGE €€

pensioneaccademia.it
This 17th-century *palazzo*, west of the Accademia, once housed the Russian Embassy. Its charming rooms are grand and furnished with antiques, although some are small. The lovely garden has a good view of the Canal Grande.
✚ E7 ✉ Fondamenta Bollani, Dorsoduro 1058 ☎ 041 521 0188 🚊 Accademia N, 1, 2

AI DUE FANALI €

aiduefanali.com
Set on a tranquil *campo* just back from the Canal Grande, yet only 10 minutes from the station and Piazzale Roma, many of this hotel's comfortable rooms have canal views. Rooms are traditionally furnished, and some are rather small, though they have terracotta and marble bathrooms. There's a roof terrace for summer breakfasts.

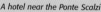E3 ⊠ Campo San Simeon Grande, Santa Croce 946 ☎ 041 718490 ⛴ Riva di Biasio 1, 5.1, 5.2

AI DUE PRINCIPI €€

hotelaidueprincipi.com
The more expensive rooms of this boutique hotel have views over Campo San Zaccaria or the canal in front; they are lofty and spacious, while the bathrooms are state-of-the-art. The public areas are chic and comfortable and breakfasts are served in a semi-minimalist room.
K6 ⊠ Fondamenta dell'Osmarin, Castello 4971 ☎ 041 241 3979 ⛴ Services to San Zaccaria

AI TOLENTINI €

albergoaitolentini.it
If you're looking for a simple, excellent-value hotel, the Tolentini, a few minutes' walk from Piazzale Roma, is a good find. The immaculately clean rooms are on the small side, but some have canal views and the beds are comfortable. Breakfast is not served, but there are bars close by. You can find

reduced advance booking rates online; prices plummet in winter.
D5 ⊠ Calle Amai, Santa Croce 197 ☎ 041 275 9140 ⛴ Services to Piazzale Roma

AL PIAVE €€

hotelalpiave.com
This 27-room hotel is located near Campo Santa Maria Formosa and offers good value for Venice. A very sleek, art deco-inspired lobby welcomes guests.
J5 ⊠ Ruga Giuffa, San Marco 4838–50 ☎ 041 528 5174 ⛴ San Marco Vallaresso, San Marco Giardinetti, Rialto N, 1, 2

CA' DOGARESSA €€

cadogaressa.com
Ca' Dogaressa is a good bet in Cannaregio, where so many hotels are on the busy stretch from the station. The hotel, on the Canale di Cannaregio, has waterside views and the decor of this 18th-century *palazzo* is traditionally Venetian, with beamed ceilings, brocade and Murano glass chandeliers. The owners go out of their way to help guests enjoy Venice.

A hotel near the Ponte Scalzi

Many hotels now occupy restored palazzi

⊞ D2 ✉ Fondamenta di Cannaregio, 1018 Cannaregio ☎ 041 275 9441
🚤 Tre Archi 4.1, 4.2, 5.1, 5.2

CA' FOSCARI €
locandacafoscari.com
This relaxed and well-appointed 1-star hotel has 10 rooms (five with private bathroom) and is hidden away in an alley.
⊞ E6 ✉ Calle della Frescada, Dorsoduro 3888/b ☎ 041 710 401 🚤 San Tomà or Ca' Rezzonico N, 1, 2

CA' MARIA ADELE €€€
camariaadele.hotelinvenice.com
Right next to the Salute and a minute's walk from the *vaporetto*, this luxurious little hotel provides the ultimate in luxurious and romantic living. Choose between one of the themed suites, where the decor ranges from cozy fireside to oriental, or relax in the comfort of a more conventional room. Breakfast is served in a charming room dominated by an over-the-top Murano glass chandelier.
⊞ G7 ✉ Rio Terrà dei Catecumeni, 111 Dorsoduro ☎ 041 520 3078 🚤 Salute

LA CALCINA €€
lacalcina.com
Overlooking the Giudecca canal in elegant Dorsoduro, this long-established hotel has classically comfortable rooms, good facilities and a lovely waterfront terrace.

NOISE
Although Venice is remarkably quiet, it still has its fair share of nocturnal traffic—even without cars. Church bells clang through the night and pedestrian chatter in the main alleys and streets is amplified in the close quarters. Traffic on the main canals can also be surprisingly noisy, and refuse boats, *vaporetti* and food suppliers start up very early. This can put a different complexion on that desirable room overlooking the Canal Grande.

⊞ F8 ✉ Fondamenta Zattere ai Gesuati and Fondamenta Vernier, Dorsoduro 780 ☎ 041 520 6466 🚤 Zattere 2, 5.1, 5.2, 6, 8

CANADA €
canadavenice.com
This immaculate 25-room hotel has several singles. The best room (a double) has its own roof terrace. Reserve in advance.
⊞ J5 ✉ Campo San Lio, Castello 5659 ☎ 041 522 9912 🚤 Rialto N, 1, 2

CENTURION PALACE €€€–€€€€
sinahotels.com
In 2009, 5-star luxury came to Dorsoduro when Palazzo Genovese opened after a lengthy restoration. Set where the Canal Grande opens out into the Bacino, the hotel fuses a sensitive recon-struction of a historic building with

SLEEP

STAYING IN VENICE TODAY
Accommodations in Venice cover everything from excessive luxury to basic, and distinctly old-fashioned, bed and breakfast-type options. With this wide choice, base your research on a category or area that appeals, and whittle it down by price, though these vary considerably depending on the season. It may be cheaper to book your trip as a package; for upper-end accommodations this will certainly be true. Self-catering is a popular option, giving you more space at lower prices; there are several online letting agencies.

21st-century taste and style.
Rooms are superbly equipped and
comfortable in a modern fashion,
while the restaurant, lounges and
bar overlook the Canal Grande.
➕ G7 ✉ Campo San Gregorio,
Dorsoduro 173 ☎ 041 34281 🚤 Salute

DANIELI €€€–€€€€
danielihotelvenice.com
A hotel since 1822, the Danieli is
the choice of visiting royalty and
VIPs. It ranks as the finest of
Venice's luxury hotels—but stay in
the old wing of the Gothic *palazzo*
rather than the newer annexe.
➕ J6 ✉ Riva degli Schiavoni–Calle delle
Rasse, Castello 4196 ☎ 041 522 6480
🚤 San Zaccaria 1, 2

DONI €
albergodoni.it
An intimate good-value 1-star
hotel between the Basilica and San
Zaccaria where some of the simple
rooms (four with bathroom) over-
look the Riva del Vin or the garden.
➕ K6 ✉ Calle del Vin, off Salizzada San
Provolo, Castello 4656 ☎ 041 522 4267
🚤 All services to San Zaccaria

FIORITA €
locandafiorita.com
This pretty, popular hotel is in a
quaint square (used for breakfast
in summer) just north of Santo
Stefano. The rooms (with private
bath) have beamed ceilings.

➕ F6 ✉ Campiello Novo, San Marco
3457/a ☎ 041 523 4754 🚤 Accademia or
Sant'Angelo N, 1, 2, 4

FLORA €€
hotelflora.it
This good-sized hotel has a well-
deserved reputation, thanks to its
pleasant garden. Some rooms are
rather small. It is just off the south
side of Calle Larga (Viale) XXII
Marzo west of Piazza San Marco.
➕ G7 ✉ Calle Bergamaschi, San Marco
2283a ☎ 041 520 5844 🚤 Giglio 1

HOTEL AMERICAN DINESEN
€€
hotelamerican.com
The American is two minutes' walk
from the Accademia, on a small
canal. Recent renovations have
brought rooms up to date and you
can expect a combination of traditional textiles and decor with
stream-lined facilities. There's a
lovely terrace for evening drinks.
➕ F7 ✉ Fondamenta Bragadin, Rio di San
Vio, Dorsoduro 628 ☎ 041 520 4733
🚤 Accademia N, 1, 2

IRIS €
hotelirisvenice.com
The Iris is in a quiet area of San
Polo near the Frari church. The
guest rooms are light and simply
furnished; not all have private
bathrooms, but each has a TV,
hairdryer and telephone.

SLEEP

RESERVATIONS
It is now almost essential to reserve a room in Venice for July and August, and wise to do
so during the rest of the peak season, which officially runs from 15 March to 15 November
and from 21 December to 6 January, and now in effect includes the period of *Carnevale* in
February. Many hotels do not recognize a low season, however, and lower category hotels
where you might have been able to negotiate lower off-season rates often close in winter.
Check out the internet for best deals.

Since 1822, when the Danieli (▷ 158) opened, Venice hasn't been short of top hotels. Plenty of new kids on the block have arrived, catering for a well-heeled, but younger and trendier crowd. Type "boutique hotels Venice" into a search engine for a wide choice. For peace and quiet consider the luxury of the Cipriani (hotelcipriani.it), set in gardens on the Giudecca island) or San Clemente Palace (sanclementepalacevenice.com), with a lagoon island to itself, pool, spa and tennis. It is connected to the city by private launch.

➕ E5 ✉ Fondamenta dei Forner, Calle del Cristo, San Polo 2910/a ☎ 041 522 2882 🚢 San Tomà

LOCANDA LA CORTE €€

locandalacorte.it

This delightful hotel was home to a Venetian noble family in the 16th century, and its rooms maintain a historic and luxurious look but with modern amenities. The inner courtyard, where breakfast is taken, is a special treat.

➕ J5 ✉ Calle Bressana, Castello 6317 ☎ 041 241 1300 🚢 Fondamente Nove 5.2

LOCANDA SILVA €

locandasilva.it

The Silva is in a lively *calle* between Santa Maria Formosa and San Marco. The public areas, including the breakfast room, have modern furniture and fittings, while bedrooms are light, modern and functional. Some have pleasant canal views and the cheapest share a bathroom.

➕ J5 ✉ Fondamenta di Remedio, Castello 4423 ☎ 041 522 7643 🚢 Services to San Zaccaria

PALAZZO STERN €€–€€€

palazzostern.com

For a room with a view, check into the Stern, one of Venice's prettiest Gothic Canal Grande *palazzi*. The breakfast terrace is set on the water; inside, an overhaul restored the interior to its Gothic-Moorish appearance, the work of the 19th-century owner. Rooms are traditionally furnished in Venetian style, and there's a rooftop jacuzzi with great city views.

➕ E6 ✉ Calle del Traghetto, Dorsoduro 2792/a ☎ 041 277 0869 🚢 Ca'Rezzonico 1

SAN SEBASTIANO GARDEN €€

hotelsansebastianogarden.com

Tucked away on a quiet canal just back from the Giudecca canal, this comfortable hotel is housed in a thoughtfully renovated old *palazzo*. All is space and calm in the public areas, while the bedrooms are large, traditionally decorated and comfortable. The chief draw, perhaps, is the lovely garden.

➕ D6 ✉ Fondamenta San Sebastiano, Dorsoduro 2542 ☎ 041 523 1233 🚢 San Basilio 2, 6, 8

LA VILLEGGIATURA €–€€

lavilleggiatura.it

It's worth the climb to the third floor to this airy, light-filled bed and breakfast, with its individually styled and spacious rooms. Wooden floors, lamps, textiles and paintings add character; bathrooms are bright and moderns. Breakfasts are ample and served in a beautifully traditional Venetian *salotto*.

➕ G4 ✉ Calle dei Botteri, San Polo 1569 ☎ 041 524 4673 🚢 Rialto Mercato 1

SLEEP

Need to Know

This section takes you through all the practical aspects of your trip to make it run more smoothly and to give you confidence before you go and while you are there.

NEED TO KNOW

Planning Ahead

WHEN TO GO

Avoid July and August, the hottest and busiest months, and plan a visit for April (excluding the busy Easter period), May, June, September or October. Hotels are busy from Easter to October, in February during Carnevale, and over Christmas and New Year. Despite the weather, winter can still be a delightful time to see the city.

TEMPERATURE

JAN	FEB	MAR	APR	MAY	JUN	JUL	AUG	SEP	OCT	NOV	DEC
43°F	46°F	59°F	66°F	73°F	74°F	79°F	79°F	70°F	61°F	54°F	45°F
6°C	8°C	12°C	15°C	20°C	23°C	26°C	25°C	21°C	16°C	12°C	7°C

Spring (March to May) has a mixture of sunshine and showers, the chilly easterly wind, the *bora*, can lower temperatures. Fog occurs occasionally.

Summer (June to August) can be unpredictable; clear skies and searing heat one day followed by sultry clouds and thunderstorms the next.

Autumn (September to November) can be glorious, though be prepared for wet days and *acqua alta* (peak tides). November is often wet and foggy with *acqua alta* (high water).

Winter (December to February) *Acqua alta* can occur at any time (including into March); January and early February can be bitterly cold with brilliant sunshine.

WHAT'S ON

February *Carnevale* (Carnival): pageants, masks and costumes.

March *Su e zo per i ponti*: A long road race in which competitors run "up and down the bridges" of Venice (fourth Sunday in Lent).

April *Festa di San Marco*: A gondola race from Sant'Elena to the Punta della Dogana marks the feast day of Venice's patron saint. Men traditionally give women a red rose.

May *La Sensa*: Venice's mayor re-enacts the Marriage to the Sea, in which the doge would cast a ring into the sea to symbolize the "wedding" of the city to the sea (Sunday after Ascension Day).

Vogalonga: Literally the "long row," a 32km (20-mile) race from Piazza San Marco to Burano and back (one Sunday in May).

June *Biennale*: Venice's international art exhibition (Jun–Nov) is in odd-numbered years; architectural Biennale in even-numbered years.

July *Festa del Redentore*: Pontoons are laid across the Giudecca canal to the Redentore to celebrate Venice's deliverance from the plague of 1576. People picnic in boats and watch fireworks (third Sunday of the month).

September *Venice Film Festival*: Held on the Lido (late Aug/early Sep).

Regata Storica: Historical costume pageant and procession of boats on the Canal Grande, followed by a race among gondoliers (first Sunday of the month).

November *Festa della Salute*: A pontoon is built across the Canal Grande, to the Salute, to celebrate the passing of a plague in 1630 (21 Nov).

VENICE ONLINE

enit.it
The main Italian Tourist Board website carries a wealth of information on everything you need to know about the whole country, with Venice getting plenty of attention. The site is available in several languages.

veneziaunica.it
Advance booking, reduced-price, official site for transportation, sightseeing and everything you'll need. Prices fluctuate according to how busy the city will be during your visit, and all services on offer are optional, enabling you to build your own package. Book seven days in advance and collect your tickets on arrival.

turismovenezia.it
This excellent site, in English and Italian, has information on every aspect of the city. You'll find details of accommodation, restaurants and shopping as well as the full lowdown on what to see and do. A frequently updated newsletter has good links to other sites.

comune.venezia.it
Although aimed as much at local residents as visitors, the city council's site provides good up-to-date information on cultural activities and historic sites in the city. Look here for the latest on erratically opening museums, city services and what's on when. The site is linked to veneziaunica.it.

venezia.net
Italian site with English version. News, general travel information, shopping, a selection of bars, cafés and restaurants, excellent material on museums and main attractions, plus 3-D tours of sights.

Venezia Unica, the app
This free interactive app contains all the information you'll need during your stay and it's updated all the time. There are maps, travel and transport details, information on culture, shopping, eating, drinking and much more.

USEFUL SITES

actv.it
Venice's city transportation system runs this informative site where you'll find full route details, timetables and fare structures for the *vaporetto* network.

trenitalia.com
The official site of the Italian State Railways with excellent train information and an easy-to-use search facility—good for forward planning.

visitmuve.it
Everything about Venice's museums, including the collections, opening times, prices and facilities.

fodors.com
A travel-planning site where you can research prices and weather, book tickets, cars and rooms, and ask fellow travelers questions; links to other sites.

INTERNET ACCESS

As well as internet access in many hotels and internet cafés, Venice now has WiFi access at hot spots all over the city, which are mapped at cittadinanzadigitale.it/node/67. To use these, pay online and obtain a username and password from veniceconnected.com. Twenty-four hour access costs €5, 72 hours €15, and seven days €20.

Getting There

ENTRY REQUIREMENTS

For the latest passport and visa information, look up the British embassy website at gov.uk/government/world/italy or the United States embassy it.usembassy.gov. EU citizens can obtain health care with the production of the EHIC card. However, insurance to cover illness and theft is strongly advised.

ARRIVING BY CAR

Cars must be left at one of the multi-story car parks at the Tronchetto. From here you can catch boat No. 2 to the rest of the city or use the People Mover, a monorail that connects the parking with Piazzale Roma in a couple of minutes, stopping en route at the cruise ship terminal. From Piazzale Roma you can walk or catch boats N, 1, 2, 3, 4.1, 4.2, 5.1, 5.2, 6. Rates start at about €32 a day (veniceparking.it). There are no free car parks and no other parking places; cars parked elsewhere will be towed away and in summer, long lines on the causeway approaching the city are common. Consider leaving your car in Mestre and then taking the train.

AIRPORTS

There are direct flights to Venice from all over the world. Venice has two main airports, Marco Polo and Canova in Treviso.

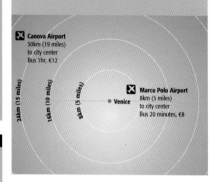

Canova Airport
30km (19 miles)
to city center
Bus 1hr, €12

24km (15 miles)
16km (10 miles)
8km (5 miles)

● Venice

Marco Polo Airport
8km (5 miles)
to city center
Bus 20 minutes, €8

FROM MARCO POLO
Scheduled internal and international flights (plus a few charters) arrive at Venice's Marco Polo Airport, 8km (5 miles) north of the city hub. For flight information, call 041 260 9260 or visit veniceairport.it. Connections from Marco Polo to Piazzale Roma take 20–40 minutes and can be made by taxi, blue ATVO Fly/35 bus (atvo.it; every 30 minutes 8.10am–11.40pm, to 12.20am on Sat; €8 one-way) or less expensive ACTV No. 5 orange city buses (actv.it; 4.08am–1.10am; €3 one-way). Buy tickets for buses from the automatic ticket machines in the baggage reclaim area, in the arrivals hall or next to the bus stop. Buses leave from the concourse outside the terminal.

BY WATER FROM SAN MARCO
There are two options: a regular boat service, run by Alilaguna, or the more expensive option, the water taxi. To get to the water terminal and boats turn left outside the main terminal building; a covered, moving walkway connects with the boat services into Venice. The cheaper option is run by the Società Alilaguna (tel 041 240 1701, alilaguna.com) with an hourly boat service from Marco Polo

to the city. It costs €15 and goes to San Marco, the Lido and Zattere. Make sure you buy your ticket before you leave the airport, the office is close to the arrivals hall exit.

ROUTES

Of the three lines, the Alilaguna Rossa goes via Murano, the Lido, the Arsenale and San Zaccaria to San Marco; and the Linea Alilaguna Blu travels via the Lido, the Arsenale, San Marco, the Zattere and the Hilton on the Giudecca to the Cruise Terminal. Choose the service that takes you closest your hotel; you may find that you will have to connect with an ACTV vaporetto for the last stages.
● The Blu (blue) services start at 6.10am; thereafter the boat leaves at 7.10, then hourly at 10 minutes past the hour until 3.15pm.
● The Rossa (red) boats start at 9.15am and run hourly until 15 minutes past midnight. Tickets cost €15 and the journey time is 75–90 minutes; the service runs Apr–Oct.
● The Arancio line runs to the Fondamenta Nove and Santa Maria del Giglio via the Canal Grande half-hourly from 7.45–7.45, then hourly till midnight throughout the year; tickets cost €15.

WATER TAXIS

Water taxis are run by the Consorzio Motoscafi Venezia, whose desk is to the left of the exit from the baggage reclaim area in the Marco Polo airport arrivals hall (tel 041 541 5084/328 238 9661; motoscafivenezia. it, veneziataxi.it). The taxis run to most points within the city (20 minutes), but the prices are high (officially €50 but baggage sur-charges can easily double this).

FROM TREVISO

Treviso airport (tel 0422 315 111 or 0422 315 1312, trevisoairport.it), 30km (19 miles) outside the city, is served by low-cost airlines; a ATVO/Eurobus shuttle (atvo.it; €12 each way) connects with some of these. Buy tick-ets at the ATVO ticket office or foreign exchange outlet.

Trains to Venice arrive at the Venezia Santa Lucia station, often abbreviated as Venezia SL (☎ 89 20 21 or 199 892 021; from outside Italy 0039 06 684 75475; tren italia.it). The station is at the head of the Canal Grande, five minutes' walk from Piazzale Roma; from the quays outside there are frequent vaporetto (1, 2 and others) and motoscafo (5.2) boat services to the rest of the city. Be sure the boat you board is heading in the right direction. Many through trains stop on the mainland at Mestre station (☎ 041 929 472), confusingly called Venezia Mestre (Venezia M), without continuing to Venice proper. Check your train is destined for Santa Lucia; if not, catch one of the frequent connecting services at Mestre for the 15-minute trip across the causeway.

Before you leave, ask your hotel to send you details of how to reach them. You need to know the nearest vaporetto stop, the name of the street as well as the numero civico (the number given after the district in the address), and the nearest landmark, such as a campo, church or museum.

NEED TO KNOW

Getting Around

VISITORS WITH DISABILITIES

Venice is difficult for visitors with disabilities. Streets are narrow, there are numerous bridges and moving on and off boats is almost impossible. Hotels, galleries and other public spaces are often in historic buildings where conservation restrictions limit access. This said, matters are improving, and the Venetian and Italian state tourist offices have lists of suitable hotels and contact details of Italian associations for those with disabilities.

GONDOLAS

Hiring a gondola is enchanting, but expensive (starting at around €80 for 40 minutes). Rates are negotiable, so confirm the cost and duration before departure. Do not be afraid to walk away or haggle if the prices seem too high and there are plenty of gondoliers. If cost is an issue take the cheap public gondolas, the *traghetti*.

The best way to move around Venice is on foot; this is how the Venetians themselves get from place to place, combining walking with the judicious use of public transportation in the shape of *vaporetti* (water buses) and *traghetti* (cross-Canal Grande ferries).

BOATS

● ACTV runs two basic types of boat: the general-purpose *vaporetto* and the faster *motoscafi*. Both follow set routes and are numbered at the front of the boat. As the same number boat may run in two directions it is vital at the quays—which have separate boarding points for each direction—to make sure you board a boat heading the right way. This is particularly true at the Ferrovia and San Zaccaria—both are busy terminals for several routes.

● The web of boat routes around Venice is not as confusing as it first seems. The basic route is Line 1 along the Canal Grande (Piazzale Roma–Vallaresso–Lido and back). Line 2 also follows the Canal Grande, but has fewer stops. A second 2 boat runs from San Zaccaria to Piazzale Roma by way of the Giudecca. The other boat you may use is the No. 12, which runs to the islands of Murano and Burano from the Fondamente Nuove. The No. 9 shuttle connects Burano and Torcello. The ferry information throughout this guide gives the nearest stop as well as the line number.

● Tickets can be bought at most landing stages, on board boats (with a surcharge), and at shops or tobacconists with an ACTV sticker. One-way tickets (€7.50, valid for 60 minutes) are valid along the length of the route so the price is the same for one stop or 10 stops. Tickets must be validated by passing them in front of the I-Mob electronic scanner before boarding; a green light will show. If you have a tourist ticket this must be validated every time you use it. There are spot fines for riding without a ticket.

● Special tickets are available (▷ panel).
● ACTV runs a less frequent service with a

reduced number of stops throughout the night on key Canal Grande routes (indicated by "N" throughout the guide). Exact times are posted on the timetables at every quay. Tickets can be bought on board.

TAXIS

● For rides to and from the mainland there are taxi stands at Piazzale Roma, tel 041 595 2080; Marco Polo Airport, tel 041 541 6363; and Mestre rail station, tel 041 936 222. Otherwise, call Radio Taxi, tel 041 5964.

TRAGHETTI

● As there are only four main bridges across the Canal Grande, Venice's *traghetti* (ferries) provide an invaluable service. Think of them as bridges and it becomes clear they will save both time and unnecessary mileage. They exist primarily for the convenience of locals, but once you are familiar with the system, judicious use of the *traghetti* will help you get quickly from point to point. Using large gondolas, they ply back and forth at seven strategic points. Quays are usually obscure, so look for the little green "Traghetto" signs. Crossings cost around €0.60, which you hand to the ferryman as you board. Venetians usually stand, but nobody minds if you sit unless the boat is crowded. Be careful with small children, and watch your balance when the boat pushes off.

WATER TAXIS

● Venice's water taxis *(motoscafi),* a fast but extremely expensive way to travel (▷ 164–165), are grouped into a co-operative of several firms, Motoscafi Venezia. A one-way transfer from the airport to Piazzale Roma costs around €100, with surcharges levied for each piece of baggage, and extra charges on public holidays and for each additional passenger over a maximum of four. The easiest, and cheapest, way to book is pre-booking on-line at motoscafivenezia.it, or by calling the central booking line on 041 541 5084.

TOURIST INFORMATION

● Main tourist offices
☎ 041 24 24
veneziaunica.it
● San Marco 🆔 H7
✉ Piazza San Marco 71/f
🕐 Daily 9–7
● Train station 🆔 D4
✉ Ferrovia 🕐 Daily 8–6.30
● Piazzale Roma 🆔 D5
✉ Vela office 🕐 Daily 10–6

LOST PROPERTY

● City streets ☎ 041 274 8225 or visit Vigili Urbani office in Pizzale Roma
● Buses or boats ☎ 041 272 2179 or 041 2424
🕐 Mon–Sat 8–6/4.30 in winter
● Train or station
☎ 041 785 531
● Report lost passports to the police and your consulate
● Report general losses to Questura, the main police
✉ Fondamenta Santa Chiara, Santa Croce 500
☎ 041 271 5511

NEED TO KNOW

Essential Facts

EMBASSIES AND CONSULATES

● Canada ✉ 3 Piazza Cavour, 20121 Milan ☎ 02 6269 4238
● France ✉ (Honorary Consul), Palazzo Morosini, Calle del Pestina, Castello 6140 ☎ 041 522 4319
● Netherlands ✉ San Vidal, San Marco 2888 ☎ 041 528 3416
● Republic of Ireland ✉ Piazza San Pietro in Gessate 2, Milano 20122 ☎ 02 551 87569
● Spain ✉ 26 Via Fatebenefratelli, 20121 Milan ☎ 02 632 8831
● UK ✉ Via San Paolo 7, 1-20121 Milan ☎ 02 723 001
● USA ✉ Via Principe Amedeo 2/10, Milano 20121 ☎ 02 290 351

ELECTRICITY

● Current is 220 volts AC (50 cycles), but is suitable for 240-volt appliances.
● Plugs are the continental two-round-pin.

EMERGENCY PHONE NUMBERS

● Emergency services (police, fire and ambulance), tel 113
● Police (Carabinieri), tel 112
● Questura (Venice Police Station), tel 041 271 5511
● Fire (Vigili di Fuoco), tel 113 or 115
● Ambulance, tel 041 523 0000 or 118
● Hospital and first aid (Ospedale Civile) at Campo SS Giovani e Paolo, tel 041 529 4111

MONEY

● The euro is the official currency of Italy. Bank notes in denominations of 5, 10, 20, 50, 100, 200 and 500 euros, and coins in denominations of 1, 2, 5, 10, 20 and 50 cents and 1 and 2 euros.
● Foreign-exchange facilities are available at banks and kiosks throughout the city. Major credit cards are widely accepted in Venice and can be used in ATMs displaying the appropriate sign.

NATIONAL HOLIDAYS

● 1 January: New Year's Day; 6 January: Epiphany; Easter Monday; 25 April: Liberation Day; 1 May: Labor Day; 2 June: Republic Day; 15 August: Assumption; 1 November: All Saints' Day; 8 December: Immaculate Conception; 25 December: Christmas Day; 26 December: Santo Stefano

OPENING HOURS

● Banks: Mon–Fri 8–1.30 (larger branches also 3–4 and restricted Sat opening).
● Churches: Non fixed hours but generally Mon–Sat 9–12, 3–6, Sun 1–5; except St. Mark's and those in the Chorus Group (▷ 4) scheme.
● Shops: Generally daily 9–1, 4–8 or 9.30/ 10–7.30/8; most food shops close Wed

afternoons except in summer; other shops close Monday mornings except in summer.

POST OFFICES

● Venice's central post office *(posta* or *ufficio postale)* is between Piazza San Marco and the Rialto at Calle delle Acque 5016 San Marco (tel 041 240 4149). There are other offices in each *sestiere* and one on the Giudecca.

● Stamps *(francobolli)* are available from post offices and tobacconists *(tabacchi)* displaying a large "T" sign.

● Mailboxes are red or blue and are marked *Poste* or *Lettere*. Blue boxes are for faster and more expensive *posta prioritaria* services only.

SENSIBLE PRECAUTIONS

● Venice's tourists are a target for theft, but with a few precautions you can stay safe. Report thefts to your hotel and then to the main police station. Report lost passports to the police or embassy.

TELEPHONES

● Telecom Italia (TI) provides public telephones in bars and on the streets. Mobile telephone reception is excellent throughout the city; TIM and Wind are the main providers. You can buy a local pay-as-you-go SIM card from their offices to keep costs down.

● Public phones accept phone cards *(schede telefoniche)*, available from tobacco shops, TI offices, automatic dispensers or stores displaying a TI sticker.

● The area code for Venice is 041 and must be used when calling from outside and within Venice.

TOILETS

● Venice has public toilets at the rail station and in larger museums. There are public toilets throughout the city marked with blue and green signs. Most cost €1.50 and some have attendants to give change if needed.

● In bars and cafés ask for *il gabinetto* or *il bagno.* Do not confuse *signori* (men) with *signore* (women).

HEALTH

● Likely hazards include too much sun, air pollution and biting insects.

● Water is safe to drink unless marked *acqua non potabile.*

● Pharmacies *(una farmacia)* are identified by a green cross and have the same opening hours as shops, but open late on some days as displayed on pharmacy doors. Staff can give advice on minor ailments and dispense many medicines over the counter, including some only available by prescription in other countries. Remember to bring any prescriptions that might be required to obtain medicine.

● If you wish to see a doctor *(un medico)*, ask at your hotel. For first aid *(pronto soccorso)* or hospital treatment, visit the Ospedale Civile ✚ J4 ✉ Campo Santi Giovanni e Paolo, Castello ☎ 041 529 4111

ETIQUETTE

● In churches do not wear shorts or miniskirts and cover your arms.

● Do not intrude while church services are in progress.

● Do not eat or drink in churches. Many churches and galleries forbid flash photography, or ban photography altogether.

Words and Phrases

All Italian words are pronounced as written, with each vowel and consonant sounded. Only the letter h is silent, but it modifies the sound of other letters. The letter c is hard (as in English "cat"), except when followed by i or e, when it becomes the soft ch of "cello." Similarly, g is soft (as in the English "giant") when followed by i or e—*giardino, gelati*; otherwise hard (as in "gas")—*gatto*. Words ending in o are almost always masculine in gender (plural: -i); those ending in a are generally feminine (plural: -e). Use the polite second person *(lei)* to speak to strangers and the informal second person *(tu)* to friends or children.

USEFUL WORDS

yes	*sì*
no	*no*
please	*per favore*
thank you	*grazie*
you're welcome	*prego*
excuse me!	*scusi*
where	*dove*
here	*qui/qua*
there	*lì/là*
when	*quando*
now	*adesso*
later	*più tardi*
why	*perchè*
who	*chi*
may I/can I	*posso*
good morning	*buon giorno*
good afternoon/ good evening	*buona sera*
good night	*buona notte*
hello/good-bye (informal)	*ciao*
hello (on the telephone)	*pronto*
I'm sorry	*mi dispiace*
left/right	*sinistra/destra*
open/closed	*aperto/chiuso*
good/bad	*buono/cattivo*
big/small	*grande/piccolo*
with/without	*con/senza*
more/less	*più/meno*
hot/cold	*caldo/freddo*
early/late	*presto/ritardo*
today/tomorrow	*oggi/domani*
when?/do you have?	*quando?/avete?*

NUMBERS

1	*uno, una*
2	*due*
3	*tre*
4	*quattro*
5	*cinque*
6	*sei*
7	*sette*
8	*otto*
9	*nove*
10	*dieci*
20	*venti*
30	*trenta*
40	*quaranta*
50	*cinquanta*
100	*cento*
1,000	*mille*

COLORS

black	*nero*
brown	*marrone*
pink	*rosa*
red	*rosso*
orange	*arancia*
yellow	*giallo*
green	*verde*
light blue	*celeste*
sky blue	*azzurro*
purple	*viola*
white	*bianco*
grey	*grigio*

EMERGENCIES

help!	*aiuto!*
stop, thief!	*al ladro!*
can you help me, please?	*può aiutarmi, per favore?*
call the police/an ambulance	*chiami la polizia/un'ambulanza*
I have lost my wallet/passport	*ho perso il portafoglio/il passaporto*
where is the police station?	*dov'è il commissariato?*
where is the hospital?	*dov'è l'ospedale?*
I don't feel well	*non mi sento bene*
first aid	*pronto soccorso*

USEFUL PHRASES

How are you? (informal)	*Come va?*
I'm fine	*Sto bene*
I do not understand	*Non ho capito*
Do you speak English?	*Parla Inglese?*
How much is it?	*Quant'è?*
Do you have a room?	*Avete camere libere?*
Can I see the room?	*Posso vedere la stanza?*
I have a reservation	*Ho una prenotazione*
How much per night?	*Quanto costa una notte?*
... with bath/shower	*... con vasca/doccia*
When is breakfast served?	*A che ora è servita la colazione?*
Where is the train/bus station?	*Dov'è la stazione ferroviaria/degli autobus*
Where are we?	*Dove siamo?*
Do I have to get off here?	*Devo scendere qui?*
I'm looking for ...	*Cerco ...*
Where can I buy ...?	*Dove posso comprare ...?*
A table for ... please	*Un tavolo per ... per favore*
I'm a vegetarian	*Sono vegetariano/a*
Is there a house specialty?	*C'è una specialità della casa?*
The bill, please	*Il conto, per favore*
We didn't have this	*Non abbiamo avuto questo*
Where are the toilets?	*Dove sono i bagni?*

DAYS/MONTHS

Monday	*lunedì*
Tuesday	*martedì*
Wednesday	*mercoledì*
Thursday	*giovedì*
Friday	*venerdì*
Saturday	*sabato*
Sunday	*domenica*
January	*gennaio*
February	*febbraio*
March	*marzo*
April	*aprile*
May	*maggio*
June	*giugno*
July	*luglio*
August	*agosto*
September	*settembre*
October	*ottobre*
November	*novembre*
December	*dicembre*

TIME AND PLACE

morning	*mattina*
afternoon	*pomeriggio*
evening	*sera*
night	*notte*
today	*oggi*
tomorrow	*domani*
yesterday	*ieri*
early	*presto*
late	*tardi*
later	*più tardi*
when	*quando*
where	*dove*
Where is...?	*Dov' è...?*
Where are we?	*Dove siamo?*
here	*qui/qua*
there	*lì/là*
near	*vicino*
far	*lontano*
on the right	*a destra*
on the left	*a sinistra*

Index

The Automobile Association would like to thank the following photographers, companies and picture libraries for their assistance in the preparation of this book.

2(i) LOOK Die Bildagentur der Fotografen GmbH/Alamy; 2(ii) Beren Patterson/Alamy; 2(iii) Nic Cleave Photography/Alamy; 2(iv) Alessandro Villa/Alamy; 2(v) imagebroker/Alamy; 3(i) AA/A Mockford & N Bonetti; 3(ii) Matthew Kawalski/Alamy; 3(iii) Kumar Sriskandan/Alamy; 3(iv) Jim Ritchie/Alamy; 4 AA/A Mockford & N Bonetti; 5 LOOK Die Bildagentur der Fotografen GmbH/Alamy; 6/7t CHRISTOPHE SIMON/AFP/Getty Images; 6ct an Dagnall/Alamy; 6cb travelstock44/Alamy; 7ct Travelshots.com/Alamy; 7cb AA/A Mockford & N Bonetti; 6/7b AA/S McBride; 8/9t Gaertner/Alamy; 8ct AA/A Mockford & N Bonetti; 8cb Alberto Paredes/Alamy; 8b petforsberg/Alamy; 9ct, 9cb AA/A Mockford & N Bonetti; 9b Food Features/Alamy; 10l AA, 10r MBP-one/Alamy; 11l AA; 11r MARKA/Alamy; 12 Beren Patterson/Alamy; 14l Paul Carstairs/Alamy; 14/15l AA/C Sawyer; 15tr, 15br AA/A Mockford & N Bonetti; 16l Peter Howard Smith/Alamy; 16/17t, 16/17b, 17r AA/A Mockford & N Bonetti; 18/19 The Art Archive/Alamy; 19r Andrea Matone/Alamy; 20l AA/S McBride; 20/21 AA/R Newton; 21r AA/C Sawyer; 22l, 22/23t, 22/23b, 23br © The Peggy Guggenheim Collection; Venice. Photo: Andrea Sarti/CAST1466; 24l, 24/25, 25tr, 25br AA/A Mockford & N Bonetti; 26/27 John Kellerman/Alamy; 27 AA/D Miterdiri; 28/29 John Kellerman/Alamy; 29tr Adam Eastland Italy/Alamy; 29br Chuck Pefley/Alamy; 30l The Art Archive/Alamy; 30/31 Hackenberg-Photo-Cologne/Alamy; 31r AA/D Miterdiri; 32l, 32tr, 32/33b, 33tl, 33r, 34 AA/A Mockford & N Bonetti; 34/35 AA/S McBride; 35 AA/A Mockford & N Bonetti; 36l © Maurizio; Cattelan/Marian Googman Gallery. Photo by Vittorio Zunino Celotto/Getty Images; 36/37c Charles Ray/Courtesy Matthew Marks Gallery, New York. Photo by Jevgenija Pigozne/Photolibrary Group; 37r Luca Da Ros/SIME/4Corners; 38l Biblio Photography/Alamy; 38/39, 39tr, 39br AA/A Mockford & N Bonetti; 40/41 Vincent MacNamara/Alamy; 41r Angelo Hornak/Alamy; 42l AA/A Mockford & N Bonetti; 42/43 AA/S McBride; 43tr, 43br AA/A Mockford & N Bonetti; 44l AA/D Miterdiri; 44tr, 44/45b AA/C Sawyer; 45tl AA/A Mockford & N Bonetti; 45r Roberto Esposti/Alamy; 46/47 AA/A Mockford & N Bonetti; 47r Worldwide Picture Library/Alamy; 48tl, 48bl, 48/49 AA/C Sawyer; 49r AA/S McBride; 50/51 AA/A Mockford & N Bonetti; 51r adam eastland/Alamy; 52l John Kellerman/Alamy; 52/53 AA/C Sawyer; 53tr, 53br AA/A Mockford & N Bonetti; 54l AA/R Newton; 54/55 AA/S McBride; 56/57 AA/A Mockford & N Bonetti; 57r Michael Harding/Alamy; 58l AA/D Miterdiri; 58/59, 59tr AA/A Mockford & Bonetti; 59br Lonely Planet Images/Alamy; 60/61 Marka/Alamy; 61tr, 61br, 62l, 62tr, 62/63, 63tl, 63c, 63r AA/A Mockford & N Bonetti; 64 Nic Cleave Photography/Alamy; 66 CuboImages srl/Alamy; 67l John Kellerman/Alamy; 67r AA/A Mockford & N Bonetti; 68l KC Hunter B/Alamy; 68r Collpicto/Alamy; 69l Stefan Nielsen/Alamy; 69r The Art Archive/Alamy; 70l F1online digitale Bildagentur GmbH/Alamy; 70r AA/A Mockford & N Bonetti; 71l Chuck Pefley/Alamy; 71r, 72 AA/A Mockford & N Bonetti; 73l David Tomlinson/Alamy; 73r; AA/A Mockford & N Bonetti; 74 Nic Cleave Photography/Alamy; 75l F1online digitale Bildagentur; GmbH/Alamy; 75r Chris Howarth/Italy/Alamy; 76 Yannis Larios/Alamy; 77 Giovanni Tagini/Alamy; 78 funkyfood London-Paul Williams/Alamy; 79 Stock Italia/Alamy; 80 Alessandro Villa/Alamy; 82t Dave Pattison/Alamy; 82b AA/A Mockford & N Bonetti; 83t Ian Dagnall/Alamy; 83b B&Y Photography/Alamy; 86(i) Chris Selby/Alamy; 86(ii) John Kellerman/Alamy; 86(iii) Julian Wyth/Alamy; 86(iv) Andrea Matone/Alamy; 86(v) Jon Arnold Images Ltd/Alamy; 88t Petr Svarc/Alamy; 88b Lonely Planet Images/Alamy; 89t Martyn Vickery/Alamy; 89c John Kellerman/Alamy; 92t Peter Barritt/Alamy; 92c Paul Carstairs/Alamy; 92b Ian Fraser/Alamy; 93 BANANA PANCAKE/Alamy; 94t Lonely Planet Images/Alamy; 94b petforsberg/Alamy; 95t Paul Carstairs/Alamy; 95c Jorge Fernandez/Alamy; 95b CuboImages srl/Alamy; 98(i) Ross Warner/Alamy; 98(ii) Craig Buchanan/Alamy; 98(iii) Adam Eastland Italy/Alamy; 98(iv) AA/A Mockford & N Bonetti; 99 Matteo Colombo/Alamy; 100t Radius Images/Alamy; 100b LOOK Die Bildagentur der Fotografen GmbH/Alamy; 101t CuboImages srl/Alamy; 101c Sarah Quill/Alamy; 104t AA/A Mockford & N Bonetti; 104c; Chuck Pefley/Alamy; 104b AA/D Miterdiri; 106t Geoff A Howard/Alamy; 106b Alessandro Villa/Alamy; 107t AA/S McBride; 107c oliver selwyn/Alamy; 107b LOOK Die Bildagentur der Fotografen GmbH/Alamy; 110(i) AA/C Sawyer; 110(ii) CuboImages srl/Alamy; 110(iii) AA/A Mockford & N Bonetti; 110(iv) imagebroker/Alamy; 110(v) AA/A Mockford & N Bonetti; 110(vi) OpenPhoto/Alamy; 110(vii) AA/A Mockford & N Bonetti; 112t I CAPTURE PHOTOGRAPHY/Alamy; 112b LOOK Die Bildagentur der Fotografen GmbH/Alamy; 113t LOOK Die Bildagentur der Fotografen GmbH/Alamy; 113b AA/A Mockford & N Bonetti; 116t giuseppe masci/Alamy; 116c Ivan Vdovin/Alamy; 116b AA/A Mockford & N Bonetti; 117 Images Etc Ltd/Alamy; 118 imagebroker/Alamy; 120/121t, 120/121ct, 120/121, 120/121cb, 120/121b AA/A Mockford & N Bonetti; 120/121b Ian Dagnall/Alamy; 121ct ENP/Alamy; 121cb AA/A Mockford & N Bonetti; 123 CuboImages srl/Alamy; 126, 130 AA/A Mockford & N Bonetti; 132/133t Cris Haigh/Alamy; 132/133ct, 132/133cb AA/A Mockford & N Bonetti; 132/133b JTB Photo Communications, Inc./Alamy; 133ct AA/R Newton; 133cb Paul Carstairs/Alamy; 138 Terry Smith Images/Alamy; 140 Matthew Kawalski/Alamy; 142t Kevin Galvin/Alamy; 142ct Bon Appetit/Alamy; 142cb Chuck Pefley/Alamy; 142b Matthias Scholz/Alamy; 145l MARKOS DOLOPIKOS/Alamy; 145r, 148 Bon Appetit/Alamy; 152 Kumar Sriskandan/Alamy; 154t David Keith Jones/Alamy; 154ct Matthias Scholz/Alamy; 154cb AA/D Miterdiri; 154b Hemis/Alamy; 156l ENP/Alamy; 156r Adam Eastland Italy/Alamy; 160 Jim Ritchie/Alamy.